RESPECT
FOR
ACTING

RESPECT
FOR
ACTING
UTA
HAGEN

with Haskel Frankel

Wiley Publishing, Inc.

Published by Wiley Publishing, Inc., New York, NY

For general information on our other products and services or to obtain technical support please contact our Customer Care Department within the U.S. at 800-762-2974, outside the U.S. at 317-572-3993 or fax 317-572-4002.

Wiley also publishes its books in a variety of electronic formats. Some content that appears in print may not be available in electronic books.

Library of Congress Cataloging-in-Publication Data: 73-2328
ISBN: 0-02-547390-5
Manufactured in the United States of America.
50 49 48 47 46

I want to thank Dr. Jacques Palaci who helped me with his scientist's knowledge in many areas in which I need further enlightenment and understanding about human motivation, behavior and psychological problems.

TO HERBERT
*who revealed and clarified
and has always set me
a soaring example*

CONTENTS

PART TWO: THE OBJECT EXERCISES

PART THREE: THE PLAY AND THE ROLE

PART
ONE
THE ACTOR

INTRODUCTION

We all have passionate beliefs and opinions about the art of acting. My own are new only insofar as they have crystallized for me. I have spent most of my life in the theater and know that the learning process in art is never over. The possibilities for growth are limitless.

I used to accept opinions such as: "You're just born to be an actor"; "Actors don't really know what they're doing on stage"; "Acting is just instinct—it can't be taught." During the short period when I, too, believed such statements, like anyone else who thinks that way, I had no respect for acting.

Many people, including some working actors, who express such beliefs may admire the fact that an actor has a trained voice and body, but they believe that any further training can come only from actually performing before an audience. I find this akin to the sink-or-swim method of introducing a child to water. Children do drown and not all actors develop by their mere physical presence on a stage. A talented young pianist, skillful at improvisation or playing by ear, might be a temporary sensation in a night club or on television, but he knows better than to attempt a Beethoven piano concerto.

THE ACTOR

The pianist's fingers just won't make it. A "pop" singer with an untrained voice may have a similar success, but not with a Bach cantata. The singer would rip his vocal chords. An untrained dancer has no hope of performing in Giselle. *The dancer would tear tendons. In their attempt they will also ruin the concerto, the cantata, and* Giselle *for themselves because, if they eventually are ready, they will only remember their early mistakes. But a young actor will unthinkingly plunge into* Hamlet *if he has the chance. He must learn that, until he's ready, he is doing the same destructive thing to himself and the role.*

More than in the other performing arts the lack of respect for acting seems to spring from the fact that every layman considers himself a valid critic. While no lay audience discusses the bowing arm or stroke of the violinist or the palette or brush technique of the painter, or the tension which may create a poor entre-chat, *they will all be willing to give formulas to the actor. The aunts and agents of the actor drop in backstage and offer advice: "I think you didn't cry enough." "I think your 'Camille' should use more rouge." "Don't you think you should gasp a little more?" And the actor listens to them, compounding the felonious notion that no craft or skill or art is needed in acting.*

A few geniuses have made their way in this sink-or-swim world, but they were geniuses. They intuitively found a way of work which they themselves were possibly at a loss to define. But even though we can't all be so endowed, we can develop a higher level of performing than the one which has resulted from the hit-or-miss customs of the past.

Laurette Taylor became a kind of ideal for me when I saw her play Mrs. Midget in Outward Bound. *Her work seemed to defy analysis. I went to see her again and again as Mrs. Midget and later as Amanda in* The Glass Menagerie. *Each time, I went to study and to learn, and each time I felt I had learned nothing because she simply caught me up in her spontaneity to the point of eliminating my own objectivity. Years later, I was excited to read the biography* Laurette *by her daughter Marguerite Courtney, and to learn that already at the turn of the century, her mother had found a way of breaking down her roles in a way which closely paralleled the principles in which I had come to believe. Laurette Taylor began her work by constructing the background of the character she was going to play. She worked for identification with this background until she believed herself to be the character, in the given circumstances, with the given relationships. Her work didn't stop until, in her own words, she was "wearing the pants" of the character! She spent rehearsals in exploring place, watching the other actors like a hawk, allowing relationships to grow, considering all possibilities for her behavior. She refused to memorize her lines until they were an integral part of her stage life. She refused to deliver fast results. She revolted against stage convention and imitation. And after all of this, she still insisted she had no technique or method of work.*

It is said that the Lunts reject "method" acting, and yet I had an experience with them that went beyond the method of most "method" actors. In the last act of Chekhov's The Sea Gull, *during the big scene between Nina and Konstantin, the rest of the household is supposed to be eating supper in the adjoining room. Mr. Lunt and Miss Fontanne worked tirelessly on this offstage supper scene, improvising dialogue, deciding what food they would be eating, searching for their behavior during this meal. In performance, when the Lunts left the stage, they actually sat down at a dinner table in the wings, ate food, chatted, and reentered with the reality of having had a meal. No one in the audience caught a glimpse of it, but they did get the clink of china and glass and silverware, and the muted offstage dialogue as a brilliant counter-*

point to the tragic onstage life. And the actors got a continuity of their existence.

Paul Muni also denied a "method" of work in developing a character. Yet in actual practice he sometimes went to live for weeks at a time in a neighborhood where his character might have lived or been born. Mr. Muni went through a process of research and work which was so deep, so subjective, that it was sometimes torturous to watch.

We may forget that Stanislavsky went to the finest actors of his day and observed them and questioned them about their approach to their work, and from these findings he built his precepts. (He didn't invent them!)

One of the finest lessons I ever learned was from the great German actor Albert Basserman. I worked with him as Hilde in The Master Builder *by Ibsen. He was already past eighty but was as "modern" in his conception of the role of Solness and in his techniques as anyone I've ever seen or played with. In rehearsals he felt his way with the new cast. (The role had been in his repertoire for almost forty years.) He watched us, listened to us, adjusted to us, meanwhile executing his actions with only a small part of his playing energy. At the first dress rehearsal, he started to play fully. There was such a vibrant reality to the rhythm of his speech and behavior that I was swept away by it. I kept waiting for him to come to an end with his intentions so that I could take my "turn." As a result, I either made a big hole in the dialogue or desperately cut in on him in order to avoid another hole. I was expecting the usual "It's your turn; then it's my turn." At the end of the first act I went to his dressing room and said, "Mr. Basserman, I can't apologize enough, but I never know when you're through!" He looked at me in amazement and said, "I'm never through! And neither should you be."*

The influences on my development, aside from the master artists I observed or worked with, have been numerous. In my parents' home, creative instincts and expression were considered worthy and noble. Talent went along with a responsibility to it. I was taught that concentrated work was a thing of joy in itself. Both my parents lived such a life and set this example for me. They also showed me that a love of work is not dependent on outward success.

I am grateful to Eva Le Gallienne for first believing in my talent, for putting me on the professional stage, for upholding a reverence for the theater, for helping me to believe that the theater should contribute to the spiritual life of a nation. I am grateful to the Lunts for endowing me with a rigorous theater discipline which is still in the marrow of my bones.

I had a strange transition from amateur to professional. The word "amateur" in its origin was a lover or someone pursuing something for love. Now it is synonymous with a dilettante, an unskilled performer, or someone pursuing a hobby or pastime. When I was very young and then when, still young, I was employed in the theater, I was an amateur in its original sense. I pursued my work for love. Then, the fact that I was paid was incidental to the love. At best, being paid meant that I was taken seriously in this love of my work. Undoubtedly I was unskilled. My strength as an actor rested in the unshakable faith I had in make-believe. I made myself believe the characters I was allowed to play and the circumstances of the characters' lives in the events of the play.

Inevitably, in the learning and turning process from amateur to professional, I lost some of the love and found my way by adopting the methods and attitudes of the "pro." I learned what I now call "tricks" and was even proud of myself. I soon learned that if I made my last exit as Nina in **The Sea Gull** *with full attention on the whys and wherefores of my leave-taking, with no attention to the effect on the audience, there were tears and a hush in the auditorium. If,* *however, I threw back my head bravely just as I got to the door, I received a round of applause. I settled for the trick which brought the applause. I could list pages of examples of acquiring "clean entrance" techniques, manufactured tears and laughter, lyric "qualities," etc.—all the things to do for calculated outer effects. I thought of myself as a genuine professional who had nothing more to learn, just other parts to make effective. I began to dislike acting. Going to work at the theater became a chore and a routine way of collecting my money and my reviews. I had lost the love of make-believe. I had lost the faith in the character, and the world the character lived in.*

In 1947, I worked in a play under the direction of Harold Clurman. He opened a new world in the professional theater for me. He took away my "tricks." He imposed no line readings, no gestures, no positions on the actors. At first I floundered badly because for many years I had become accustomed to using specific outer directions as the material from which to construct the mask for my character, the mask behind which I would hide throughout the performance. Mr. Clurman refused to accept a mask. He demanded me in the role. My love of acting was slowly reawakened as I began to deal with a strange new technique of evolving in the character. I was not allowed to begin with, or concern myself at any time with, a preconceived form. I was assured that a form would result from the work we were doing.

During the performance of the play, I discovered a new relationship to the audience which was so close, so intimate, that I thanked Harold Clurman for breaking down the wall which had so often separated me from the audience.

I went on to explore more deeply with Herbert Berghof what I had begun to learn from Harold. Herbert gave me painstaking help in how to develop and make use of these

8

discoveries, how to find a true technique of acting, how to make a character flow through me.

The American theater poses endless problems for any actor who wants to call himself an artist, who wants to be part of an art form. From the very beginnings of "doing the rounds" of agents, producers and directors; through the terrifying audition procedures; to the agonies of attempting to prove yourself, in early rehearsals; to the sense of compromise you feel in yourself, your fellow actors, the playwright, from the first rehearsal through the out-of-town tryouts to the opening night in New York; to the acceptance of the public and the critics; to the element of speculating about whether you will close on Saturday or work for years, or possibly never work again—these things make for conditions which periodically have disillusioned me about the Broadway theater, about my own work, about directors, about playwrights, about management, about every phase of my chosen profession. The only place where I have known a degree of fulfillment is at the HB Studio, where I am both teacher and learn from others.

I am lucky to have found this place where I can put a degree of my struggle for growth, my search for the miracle of reality in acting into practice. The HB Studio was founded by my husband, Herbert Berghof. We both teach there. We act there with our students and other fellow actors. We direct there. We work on plays and scenes which the commercial theater cannot afford or will not foster.

As a teacher, in view of the pages that follow, let me state what to me is not modest, but obvious. I am not an authority on behaviorism or semantics, not a scholar, a philosopher, nor a psychiatrist, and I am frankly fearful of those who profess to teach acting while plunging into areas of actors' lives that do not belong on a stage or in a classroom. I teach acting as I approach it—from the human and technical prob-

lems which I have experienced through living and practice.

I believe in my work and in what we are doing at the HB Studio. I pray that with patience and foresight a first-rate acting company will develop out of the Studio, a company guided by first-rate young directors, and, hopefully, young playwrights. When this happens, it will be a company of people who have grown together, who are united by common aims and by a way of work which has a common language and results in a homogeneous form of expression. The four walls to house such a group will follow, and then perhaps we will be able to make a real contribution to the American theater. But should it never happen, it will still be a goal worth working for!

1

CONCEPT

IF YOU HAVE the opportunity to visit the Museum of Modern Art in New York City when they are showing the film series "Great Actresses," you will see performances by Sarah Bernhardt and Eleonora Duse among others. Both actresses lived and acted at the same time; both were considered great. Yet their approach to acting differed. Sarah Bernhardt was a flamboyant, external, formalistic actress, reflecting the fashion of her time. Duse was a human being on stage. Today, Bernhardt's mannerisms make you laugh. Duse moves you; she is more modern than tomorrow.

I mention these two ladies from the past in a book meant for the actor of today because they represent two approaches to acting that have been debated in the theater through the centuries. The two approaches have names that annoy and confuse me, but since you will hear them again and again, let me name them now, and hopefully get rid of them. One is the Representational (Bernhardt), the other the Presentational (Duse).

The Representational actor deliberately chooses to imitate or illustrate the character's behavior. The Presentational actor attempts to reveal human behavior through a use of himself, through an understanding of himself and consequently an understanding of the character he is portraying. The Representational actor finds a form based on an objective result for the character, which he then carefully watches as he executes it. The Presentational actor trusts that a form will result from identification with the character and the discovery of his character's actions, and works on stage for a moment-to-moment subjective experience.

For an example of the above, let me again refer to Bernhardt and Duse. Each, in her native tongue, had played the same popular melodrama of the time, the high point of which was the moment when the wife, accused of infidelity by her husband, swore her virtue. "Je jure, je jure, JE JUUUUURE!" Bernhardt proclaimed in a rising vibrato of passion. Her audience stood to scream and shout its admiration. Duse swore her virtue softly and only twice. She never spoke the third oath, but placed her hand on her young son's head as she looked directly at her husband. Duse's audience wept.

One night, after having received accolades for his performance from the audience, the nineteenth-century French actor Coquelin called his fellow actors together backstage and said: "I cried real tears on stage tonight. I apologize. It will never happen again." His approach to acting was obviously Representational. For him, a genuine experience on stage was rejected in the belief that it would muddy or blur the acting.

I believe that the illustration of a character's behavior at the cost of removing one's own psyche, no matter how brilliant the performance that results, creates an alienation between audience and actor. The audience may yell "Bravo!," they may even rise to their feet and cheer, but they are reacting in the same manner they would to an acrobat or a high-wire performer—they are cheering the visible skill, they are applauding the feat pulled off. But the vital empathy with human behavior, the emotional involvement between actor and audience will be lacking.

Formalized, external acting (Representational) has a strong tendency to follow fashion. Internal acting (Presentational) rejects fashion and consequently can become as timeless as human experience itself.

I think now you know where I stand. Certainly it is with the Duse who, once accused of being too much alike in each of her roles, answered that as an artist the only thing she had to offer was the revelation of her soul. But if I stand with Duse and with the Presentational approach to acting, I do not reject *in toto* the Representational. To do so would be to reject actors of brilliance who have found their way along that path. I reject the Representational only for myself, as actress and teacher. I must work on an approach to the theater that functions for me. As a teacher I can teach only what I believe.

For a would-be actor, the prerequisite is *talent*. You can only hope to God you've got it. Talent is an amalgam of high sensitivity; easy vulnerability; high sensory equipment (seeing, hearing, touching, smelling, tasting—*intensely*) ; a vivid imagination as well as a grip on reality; the desire to communicate one's own experience and sensations, to make one's self heard and seen.

Talent alone is not enough. Character and ethics, a point of view about the world in which you live and an education, can and must be acquired and developed.

Ideally, the young actor should possess or seek a thorough education in history, literature, English linguistics (foreign languages are so much gravy) , as well as all of the other art forms—music, painting and dance—plus theater history and orientation.

Essential to a serious actor is the training and perfecting of the outer instrument—comprising his body, his voice and his speech. This instrument is the violin on which he will play. He should be aware that it can be comparable to a Stradivarius and that he must turn it into and treat it like one.

Since voice, speech and body work are not in my realm as a teacher, I must simply assume that any actor serious enough to read this text will never cease to develop his physical capacities through dancing, fencing, gymnastics, etc., or work for the mastery of voice production and correct standard speech. All parts of his instrument should be limber enough to respond to the psychological and emotional demands he may make on it when he springs into physical and verbal action in the character in the play. A young actor who fails as Romeo—no matter how brilliant his inner technique—because he hasn't been able to shed his Brooklyn speech or his pigeon-toed walk, has only his own laziness to blame.

Physical beauty is not a prerequisite to becoming an actor. Few of our present-day stars are physically beautiful in the conventional sense. However, the best of them, men and women, can create beauty for an audience. If you think of a beautiful baby you may remember that it graciously accepts the admiration which comes to it voluntarily. The homely baby must reach out to others and quickly learns from necessity to clown and do a hundred things to win attention. The homely baby learns what the actor must learn to say through his art, "Here I am, look at me!" The physically beautiful actor is often cursed with the passivity of easy conquest. He accepts and expects everyone to come to him, instead of reaching out to them.

Mental brilliance is not essential. An intellectual actor can intellectualize himself out of real acting impulses, while his less mentally endowed brother, provided he is not dull and insensitive, may function magnificently if he has under-standing of human behavior. (By this I do not mean to imply that if you are highly intelligent or exquisitely beautiful you don't stand a chance in the theater.)

It is necessary to have a point of view about the world which surrounds you, the society in which you live; a point of view as to how your art can reflect your judgment.

To rebel or revolt against the status quo is in the very nature of an artist. A point of view can result from the desire to change the social scene, the family scene, the political life, the state of the ecology, the conditions of the theater itself. Rebellion or revolt does not necessarily find its expression in violence. A gentle, lyric stroke may be just as powerful a means of expression. To portray things the way they are, to hold up a mirror to the society, can also be a statement of rebellion. You must ask yourself, "How can I bring all of this to the statement I wish to make in the theater?"

When you have decided what it is you wish to express, you must decide what kind of a theater you would ideally want to be a part of. And now your real problems begin!

Many other fields of artistic endeavor offer the choice of working as an artist or as a commercial craftsman. As it stands now, our theater is by its very set-up commercial. The finest and deepest play on Broadway has been produced to make money, not just to serve, enlighten or enrich the lives of those fortunate enough to afford the price of a ticket. If the play *does* serve, that's so much velvet and extremely rare. If you have decided to become a commercial actor (an honorable profession to which I attach no stigma) you will have endless practical problems in the theater, television and films. But if you want to be a serious theater artist, these problems will be multiplied endlessly by emotional frustrations, guilts and longings.

In the late 1950's, Jean Louis Barrault complained about

the theater in France. He said that it was too much like Broadway in that the theaters were becoming like garages. At first I thought he meant dirty and overcrowded. Then I realized he meant the theaters were simply being hired as space to park in for a while, instead of representing *your* theater, *your* home with its own identity where all of the productions should express your point of view about the world in which you live; in which you could even reveal your soul (Duse) through art.

Barrault had a romantic, liberal, slightly mystical point of view in his own *Theatre* which manifested itself in his choice of plays and his conception for presentation, as opposed to, let's say, the Socialist, political *Theatre Nationale Populaire* of Jean Villard and Gérard Philipe, or the traditional, academic approach of the *Comédie Française.* All three subsidized theaters played simultaneously in Paris for many years along with other groups who had their own points of view. Sometimes, more than one theater produced the same play at the same time, but each with its own distinct viewpoint. Barrault feared that these individualistic theaters were threatened by the "commercial" circumstances encroaching on the Parisian theatrical scene.

In America we don't even know what Barrault feared. Our theater with a point of view isn't threatened because it has never existed except in the minds of individual artists. Consequently, we have no true theater-going tradition. The theater is still not a part of our lives, not a necessity, not a sustenance for our spiritual lives. We actors have never had a "home" as Barrault understood it.

West Germany has over 275 subsidized repertory theaters, and West Germany is smaller than the state of Wisconsin. Its theaters are subsidized by the state, the municipality, industry and labor. The people *expect* this subsidy. They revere and honor the artist who serves in the theater—for a living wage, but not huge amounts of money. In America, our audiences, friends, families and neighbors think we are no good if we work for less than fortunes. Yet, surely, the compensation of respect is far greater than money.

In the United States, we have had a number of theaters with a point of view that almost made it—or they made it for several years. Many years ago we had the Provincetown Players, the early Theatre Guild, the Civic Repertory and the Group Theater. Since then, each decade has brought us further attempts in the establishment of meaningful and permanent companies. I'm sure you are familiar with many of them. The eventual failure of these noble ventures has almost always been connected with the success of one or more individuals who scored and then left to go on to a personal success in a film or commercial play. The venture that had served them was left behind, just a launching pad to be abandoned by those who had used it to reach personal heights. The potential of these theaters was devoured by the commercial theater.

Countless other ventures have wondered why they failed to acquire their own audiences. Their purpose is often simply to do "good" plays. Usually they present these good plays without any point of view reflecting the problems of the day. They should stop wondering and make their own statement. They will find their audience.

To maintain one's ideals in ignorance is easy; to maintain them with the full realization of the existing circumstances is not. To accept "the way it is" is the opportunistic way out or the way of the ostrich; to attempt to battle it takes knowledge and character.

I have often heard both professional, working actors and young beginners proclaim with passion, "I want to be the *best* actor in America!" But what is that? Merely a statement of a competitive goal. It epitomizes the American disease of ambition for success—accompanied by fame and fortune—as proof of worth. Steak, chicken, lobster, lamb are all delicious but which is *best?* One may be the favorite of a certain group, but others have a different preference. Who is *best* among Haydn, Mozart, and Beethoven? These three musical giants worked and created in Vienna at the same time. We may prefer the music of one composer to that of another, but there is no *best.* Each worked to create his *own* best, not to be *the* best.

A prominent actress once said to me: "I get so confused. Who am I trying to reach? The gas-station attendant or Brooks Atkinson?" She didn't understand that they both have needs for an offering, for sustenance. I explained to her that I was confused for a while when I got rave reviews in *The Sea Gull.* They went straight to my head and stayed there until I attended a matinee of another young actress who had received equally good reviews. In my judgment her performance was poor. I was forced to reevaluate my thinking. If I dismissed the critical raves for one actress, what value could I place on my own? Who, ultimately, outside myself and a few of my peers whose opinion I valued, was to be the judge of my work? I began to learn to work for standards designed neither for the gas-station attendant nor Brooks Atkinson, but for my own. Set your own goals, set them for your own approval, and those of your colleagues whom you truly respect.

By the very nature of our profession we seem to develop slothful rather than disciplined habits. A great dancer to his last days cannot—and will not—perform without hours of daily practice. The pianist Artur Rubinstein and the violinist Isaac Stern cannot—and will not—play a concert without daily practice. While an actor may be forced to work as a waiter or a typist to sustain himself while waiting for the call to play King Lear, there is no excuse for his frittering away the hours that belong to him—and his true work—with partying, and fun and games.

Every actor must demand total discipline of himself if he really means to be an actor. It can be acquired if it's not already in his bones. A very gifted actor may be surpassed and outrun by a lesser talent simply because he is lazy, buckpassing, superficial—an actor settling for the easiest choices. The less-talented actor can win with a thorough, backbreaking discipline in his work, in his examination of his materials and his relationship to it, in the dedication (that much-abused word) to his work.

Let me say something about ethics in the theater. Another reason for the collapse of well-intentioned venture after venture is sloth and egomania. We must accept that the theater is a communal adventure. Unlike the soloist we can't perform alone in the theater. (Only Ruth Draper, the monologuist, was able to do that.) The better the play, the more we need an ensemble venture. We must recognize that we need each other's strengths, and the more we need each other's professional comradeship, the better the chance we have of making theater. We must serve the play by serving each other; an ego-maniacal "star" attitude is only self-serving and hurts everyone, including the "star."

We must aim for "character" in the moral and ethical sense of the word, compounded of the virtues of mutual respect, courtesy, kindness, generosity, trust, attention to the others, seriousness, loyalty, as well as those necessary attributes of diligence and dedication.

Often a young actor reads that John Barrymore or Laurette Taylor was a heavy drinker, and decides that this is what made them successful, and so begins boozing it up. Or he may cloak himself in the exhibitionism of another star, or the vanity of still another, thinking that these detrimental traits are the key to success. I believe that personal vanity is a disease like alcoholism, or a cancer which can eat up the initial talent and sensitivity and capacity of an individual actor. Self-glorification and narcissism block the spontaneous behavior, the genuine give-and-take of any actor. Guard against it the way you would any other destructive disease.

Unfortunately, our theater has few examples on which an aspiring actor can pattern himself. Most of them seem to show us that the actor who serves himself in the play *can* succeed. This must make, and has made, for chaos in the American theater as a whole. If we want a theater to be respected in America, a theater which is needed, we must each make ourselves personally responsible, far more than in a country where the actor already has a "home." Now we are migrant workers, fruit pickers working where we are momentarily wanted and being exploited and then moving on. We have many of the same emotional and character problems of other migrant workers.

Stanislavsky's statement is always with me: "Love the art in yourself, not yourself in the art."

I vividly remember a conversation years ago involving the brilliant French actor Gérard Philipe and some American actors, myself included. We were all envious of his position in the *Theatre Nationale Populaire*—envious of his being in a position to choose the kind of theater with which he wanted to align himself, the permanence of that theater, and what it represented to the nation as a whole. One actor screamed in frustration, "We *can't* have that kind of theater in America!"

Philipe answered quietly, "That is your fault."

I knew he was correct, but it has taken me many years to define in which way. Actors are as responsible as any other group in the theater for its present state. We continuously mouth our objections and our revolt against the status quo *individually*, but we feed the status quo *collectively*. If we realize our individual responsibilities to an art form, we must not only live up to it as individuals, but remember the collective form of this art, and that more than anything else it is one for all and all for one.

I have referred to specific examples of European theaters and European artists in order to avoid direct criticism of the home scene. Despite evidence to the contrary, I refuse to believe that the American theater in all of its branches—Broadway, off-Broadway, repertory companies, regional theater—is incapable of change, revolt, or a development into true service to its public.

2

IDENTITY

If WE ARE now in agreement and have taken sides with the actor who presents rather than *re*presents; if we understand the necessity for developing an organic inner technique as well as our outer instrument; if we are convinced that a deep sense of ethics, a development of our best character elements is essential for us to become fine artists who can serve and enlighten an audience about the human experience, then the question can be asked: "Where do we begin?"

First, you must learn to know who *you* are. You must find your own sense of identity, enlarge this sense of self, and learn to see how that knowledge can be put to use in the characters you will portray on stage. I assume that most of you are, at this point, *theoretically* on my side, even though, through your previous training and experience as both actor and audience, you are still caught up in the mistaken notion that you are a human being in the wings and an "actor" on stage. You have a tendency to copy what you have seen others do on a stage, rather than to search within your own life experience to bring forth a new human being on stage.

Let us assume you are cast as Horatio in *Hamlet*. At the

mere mention of the part, each of you already has a ready-made image based on other Horatios you have seen. I doubt that it is a Horatio who has ever eaten, slept, washed, or gone to the bathroom. This doesn't mean that your Horatio will necessarily do any of these things during the course of the play—but he should be considered as a human being, not as a rubber-stamp copy of another actor.

Think of all the classical plays that have been almost buried for contemporary audiences by bad traditional acting. Why should every lady-in-waiting move like a ballet dancer? Why should every spear-carrier stand as rigid as cardboard? Why should the king and queen intone like bad opera singers without music? Where are the real human beings in these plays? They are lost behind ready-made, false forms.

But if we accept that the reality of these characters is not arrived at through the memory of other performances or through cliché generalities—royalty is imperious, courtiers are graceful, jesters are comic, spear-carriers are erect—we must also accept the converse, that realities often relied on by the supposedly "modern" actor, such as Brooklyn speech, head scratching, belching, and blue-jean postures, will not bring about a Horatio who is a close friend to a prince of Denmark, who attended the University of Wittenberg centuries ago, who is accustomed to life at court, etc. Since we cannot find reality in either of these directions, we must admit that we have not learned enough about human beings, or about *ourselves* as human beings to bring about a genuine life for these characters.

We also seem to find cliché forms for contemporary characters. We shuffle and mumble and imitate the "naturalistic" actors of today who have made a success. We look for the ordinary rather than the extraordinary in our daily lives, and so the explorations of ourselves become smaller and of less importance as we go along. We pigeonhole and characterize our behavior until our very self-image becomes as much a cliché or stereotype as does our preconception of the characters we want to play.

Our sense of reality is limited. We look at our daily lives for convenient, recognizable behaviorisms to transfer to the stage. Yet, every day some incident occurs that causes us to say: "Wow! If you saw that on a stage you wouldn't believe it." Or you, yourself, will do something unusual, and also remark, "If I did that on stage, no one would believe it." And so we water down the truth to make our stage life "natural"— whatever that's supposed to mean—even as we admit that two truck drivers, cutting in on each other and leaping to the street to have it out, are often more dramatic than Macduff besting Macbeth.

My own self-image in a given situation, who I *think* I am, is not always what I *really* am, consequently the inner image of myself in that situation may differ from the outer image I present. I *think* I'm a child of nature, open, frank, impulsive, generous, compassionate, bursting with humor, tender, brilliant, and noble. This inner image is accompanied by an image of how I think I look. I see myself striding through the countryside, shiny, with flying hair, wide-eyed, and expectant. Yet, if I walk down the street and inadvertantly catch a glimpse of myself reflected in a store window I am appalled at what I actually see.

Obviously, if the inner and outer images we have of ourselves are each as one-sided as these, we will believe that we cannot find the necessary components of another character in ourselves. We will be convinced that we can only play characters, who don't fit these images, by *illustrating* them. The more an actor develops a full sense of his own identity, the more his scope and capacity for identification with other characters than his own will be made possible.

If I compare myself to a large, meaty, round apple, I

discover that my inner and outer cliché image of myself is only a wedge of it—possibly the wedge with the rosy cheek on the skin. But I have to become aware of myself as the total apple—the firm inner flesh as well as the brown rotten spot, the stem, the seeds, the core. All of the apple is *me*. The more I discover, the more I realize that I have endless sources within myself to put to use in the illumination of endless characters in dramatic literature; that I am compounded of endless human beings depending on the events moving in on me, my surrounding circumstances, relationships with a variety of people, what I want and what's in my way at a given moment: all within the context of my unique identity.

You spontaneously play a variety of different roles in life. Imagine yourself attending a cocktail party given for producers, agents, directors, all in a position to employ you. How you feel, how you dress, how you behave will be a you that is different from the you who goes to a party of friends and colleagues in a loft where you sit guzzling wine and beer, and munching on pretzels. Or the you who attends a children's birthday party, or a party given by your parents for their friends. In each situation your very idiom changes, your self-image changes.

Assume you are at your desk writing a letter. The doorbell rings. Your self-image will change depending on whom you expect to be there. A fellow actor (which particular one?), an old friend from your home town, the superintendent, the laundryman, a parent, your agent—for each person you will present a different you.

Previous circumstances and existing circumstances will bring about a different you: whether you had a good night or a bad night, whether it is hot or cold, whether you are in a tidy or a messy state. Even something as elementary as the clothes you wear can make you feel (and then behave) old or young, a slob or elegant, awkward or in command, snobbish or humble. A confrontation with the same person, depending on your immediate desire, can make you stubborn or giving, vicious or kind, courageous or cowardly. We must learn to understand and accept the facets of ourselves which we don't wish to recognize—shyness, selfishness, greed, envy, panic, lack of control, stupidity, etc.—and, in admitting to them, enlarge our capacity for identification. Above all, we must become self-observant enough not only to recognize our needs and define our feelings, but to connect them to the behavior which ensues.

If we get into a violent argument with a bus driver, we know how we *felt,* but we rarely know how we behaved. In an encounter with a lover, we can describe our feeling of tenderness and such obvious behavior as an embrace, but the small actions that surrounded it are forgotten.

If I am to play a silly, fluffy creature, and I think I am not such a person, I cannot use myself. I mistakenly believe I can only *indicate* what *she* would do. Yet if I watch myself greeting my dogs with gushes of baby talk and little giggles, *I* am silly. If I talk to a scientist, even to an electrician, *I* am stupid, though my cliché image tells me I am brilliant. If a drunken, bigoted doorman gives me a hard time, I appear snobbish and I pull rank, though my self-image tells me I am a humanist, a liberal at all times. I think I am fearless, yet you should see me with a mouse.

The continuing job of learning to find out who you *really* are, of learning to pinpoint your responses—and even more important, the myriad, consequent behaviorisms which result—will help you begin to fill your warehouse with sources upon which to draw for the construction of a character (the new *you* selected for your character on stage). The Object Exercises, from chapters 11 through 20 are designed, among other things, to help you develop this self-awareness.

Many doubts continue to arise in both the young and

older professional, as well as in the learning actor for whom the concept of using himself primarily as the source for the stage character is relatively new. A prominent film actress, whom I was once helping with a role, was thrown by the fact that her part was just an ordinary American woman like herself—same age, background, schooling, emotional problems, etc. She felt she had nothing "to act." Her previous orientation to acting consisted of finding a mask to hide behind. She believed that the outer dressing of the part—age difference, historic difference, national difference—contained the real essence of acting. For her, acting was only a craft when it was miles away from her, and when it was used to illustrate something totally different from herself. She knew so little of herself and her own behavior that she was unable to make any use of her *self*, to strip to her soul. She had only one wish: to put on a mask, to disguise herself.

To seem to want or need a mask behind which to bury one's self often comes, not only from an incorrect concept, but from a distrust in ourselves. We harbor the suspicion that we ourselves are boring, and that only the character in the play is sufficiently interesting to hold an audience.

I like to make the example of observing a live animal on stage. Even though the actors are in the midst of strong dramatic action, the audience will be riveted on a cat, sitting quietly in a chair, following a bit of blowing lint with its eyes. Now, a cat *cannot* be as fascinating as a human being! But the cat's sensory apparatus is more powerful than a human's, and it is more single-minded in its purpose, with no mental distractions to blur its instincts. The cat really exists with strong, spontaneous, forward-moving attention, and so it can surpass the actor, who is *predictably* busy with his stage life.

I refuse to let a cat win! I know I am more interesting, but I can learn from the cat to develop my sensory apparatus, and that I should aim for the same unanticipated involvement of the moment—will I or won't I pounce? It sounds simple, but the *art* is that I can aim for that cat's spontaneity and execute it by design. What is boring is *not* the real you in action, but the *mechanical* execution of a task—whether it be overdimensional or tiny.

"If I must use myself, won't I be the same in every part I play?" The question calls to mind the "personality" actor who is *really* the same in every part he plays. Examples of this type clog the stage, screen and television. Because they are always the same does not mean that they are truly using themselves. They are simply playing the identical few notes in themselves over and over again without a real search or selection from themselves. Often, after an initial success, these "personality" actors simply copy from themselves, imitating moments and effects which have worked for them before. They rely on a quality which they feel has worked with an audience, and end up playing "the manner of" themselves in as tiresome a way as another actor playing "the quality of" the character.

One of the greatest compliments I ever received was from someone who had seen me in about ten plays, in parts as different as Saint Joan, Blanche in *A Streetcar Named Desire*, Martha in *Who's Afraid of Virginia Woolf*, and Natalya in Turgenev's *A Month in the Country*. He wanted to meet me because he couldn't figure out what I was really like. He thought I was so different in every part. And yet, while playing, after having discovered myself in the part, I always felt that it was *me* on stage in the given circumstances, not *she*.

In an interview, Ingrid Bergman once stated that when she played *The Visit* she was faced with a vengeful character whom she understood, but that vengeance was not a part of her own personality. That might be true and accurate in her private life where she has learned to control it. But it's also true that any child has experienced a sense of vengeance, even expressed it against a parent or another toddler. That your need for vengeance may not have the consequent actions of the lady in *The Visit* is not important, but that you are aware that you have experienced the need for it *is*.

Someone working on Laura in *The Glass Menagerie* will state flatly, "But I've never been shy." I have only to suggest a time when she may have been to a high school dance with a big pimple on her chin, and the memory will turn the unshy actress into a blushing wallflower.

Your own identity and self-knowledge are the main sources for any character you may play. Most human emotions have been experienced by each of us by the time we are eighteen, just as they have been by all human beings throughout the ages. That you gain control and understanding of them as you get older, that they may ease or intensify is self-evident. We do not have to get psychoanalytical or delve into Freud, Jung, Reich or Adler to learn to understand ourselves and others to be healthy artists. We have to be truly *curious* about ourselves and others!

Other questions which arise on the subject of our own limited sense of self and self-expression come from our social backgrounds, particularly middle-class America. In sections of the country we are shaped by a society which is ashamed of spontaneous emotion: "Don't cry," "Don't laugh so loud," "Don't hug me in public," "Don't scream," etc. So, obviously, when we want a genuine emotional release on stage we have a harder time uncovering it than someone who comes from a so-called "lower" class where spontaneous emotion is allowed a free reign.

The sense of identification with history is almost nil in America because history and heritage are so little respected. The Mark Twain house in New York City is pulled down and replaced by a steakhouse because our opulent society can't seem to raise the $20,000 needed to maintain it as a museum. Something similar occurs in the nation every week. This lack of respect for the past and seeming worship for innovation is a detriment to the actor. Our imagination is not stimulated by our past. (Not even by nature or the very earth we walk on.)

But if we visit England, or any other European country for that matter, we start to identify with another century on the very cobblestones. It's hard to visit the Tower of London without becoming acutely aware that those strange lives in history books lived and breathed—still seem to—in every cell, corner, and courtyard. The actor's imagination is stimulated into identification with country and period.

Historic distances fade, seemingly fictional facts become a reality if one is as lucky as I was at the age of nine to spend a summer in a medieval castle on the Rhine. The fantasies I experienced amidst towers and turrets, a real moat and a drawbridge, dungeons, ramparts—the works—allowed me to believe that I had lived for a short while in the Middle Ages.

If you can't go abroad, or even visit places like Independence Hall in Philadelphia, or Salem, Massachusetts, or other historic spots to find a variety of historical experiences, you can still read biographies and histories. Read them until you *know* you've lived in those rooms with those people, eaten that particular food, slept in that strange bed behind those curtains; danced, jousted and tilted with the best of them. (Read *Walden* and you'll understand pollution.)

Customs, architecture, fashion, social needs, politics—all change, all come and go, but throughout history people have breathed, slept, eaten, loved, hated and had similar feelings, emotions, needs. Anything which allows for a realization of this by the actor is vital. It must be grasped fully so that if, on stage, you live now or at any other time in history, you will be able to put yourself there rather than be reduced to an illustration of doing what "they" did then.

Lately, through biographies, I went to the block with Marie Antoinette in *The Fatal Friendship*. I was married to Kaiser Franz Joseph in *The Lonely Empress*. I prepared myself for the block, dressing all in red so the blood wouldn't show, as Mary, Queen of Scots, and I had all of Queen Victoria's endless children. (I also built myself a cabin in Concord!)

Keep pace with the present. Take a trip to the moon. Envision the future.

When you look at paintings, put yourself *into* them instead of looking *at* them.

The normal procedure of identifying with observed events which we went through as children should not ever stop for the adult actor. When, as children, we visit sick persons and put ourselves into their bed, fantasize their agonies, are brave and enjoy their flowers, we are simply extending our own experiences imaginatively. If we peek into a tenement window and see a drunken father abusing wife and children, we *put* ourselves there to take abuse with courage. As an adult, don't con yourself out of these fantasies. Anything which strengthens your faith that it happened to you is of use.

We must overcome the notion that we must be *regular*. ("Be like one of us." "Don't put on airs." "Don't get so fancy.") It robs you of the chance to be extraordinary and leads you to the mediocre. This insistence on conformity, on being like everyone else, often prevents us, for instance, from potentially training something as practical as our speech. Our friends and relatives castigate us as our speech improves and we try to lose dialects and regional speech hang-ups. ("What's the matter with you? You talk so stagey.") When our need to express ourselves verbally, to *truly* communicate, goes *beyond* "Cool, man!," "Wow," "Out of sight!," "It's heavy" or whatever the current slang, we are accused of artificiality. But if we listen to our friends and relatives, and stay "regular," when we approach plays of language—Shakespeare, T. S. Eliot, Fry, Shaw—we find an unfamiliarity with the verse, and the idiom makes us feel "affected." We must learn to balk at this social dictum in order to enlarge our imagination and our use of self. (Remember that vowels and consonants spat out represent our wishes.)

There is a decided difference between the self-awareness that is vital to the theater artist and the self-consciousness that is ordinarily applied to the awkward or affected person. To become aware of usually subconscious and intuitive, spontaneous behavior in order to make use of it for creating a character in a play *will not* make you self-consciously affected or unreal. Nor will it, as I have been asked, block intuitive or spontaneous behavior in our daily experiences. I am not a scientist, a psychologist or a behaviorist, but I *know* this is true.

If you are affected in your daily life, calculatingly self-aware in your relations with others, you will undoubtedly be a bad actor, because your attention is narcissistic. If you have acquired these affectations in your teens and have not shaken them by the time you are twenty, you are in trouble. After all, if you possess borrowed behavior in life and focus on *it* rather than on others, how can you be really active on stage?

When I speak of copying or imitating what you have already seen, there is a point in the life of any young artist in any art form when someone he comes in contact with, whom he idolizes, influences him so strongly that the need to emulate is almost a reflex, almost a subconscious procedure. This is true of the most gifted artist, and I suppose one way in which the finger of genius touches the next generation. This passing on down of our gifts, which we have been given by those before us, is not to be belittled or minimized. We must pray that we are influenced by the best. But try to inherit the inner work and not the outer shape (the concept, not the form). We must pray that our intuitive taste and judgment will allow us to copy—however, only temporarily—a master rather than just a momentary box-office success. Mozart was influenced by Haydn, but Mozart went on to become Mozart, and I recognize him no matter what new musical invention he has made. Beethoven was influenced by Haydn and Mozart, but found his own expression, so I recognize him in quartet, mass, or symphony. Can't we aim for that as actors? Even as *re*-creators? In finding and strengthening our own identity, can't we develop our capacity for identification to the point where we will be able to put it to service by revealing the human being in dramatic literature?

3

SUBSTITUTION

THE EXPRESSION "to lose yourself" in the part or in the performance, which has so often been used by great artists in the theater, has always confused me. I find it much more stimulating to say that I want "to find myself" in the part. To oversimplify, these artists obviously meant that one should reject the desire to show off, that one should not wallow in one's own ego, that one should not trade on personal tricks. Instead, one should become involved with the performance without concern for its outer form, pyrotechnics or personal sale.

Once we are on the track of self-discovery in terms of an enlargement of our sense of identity, and we now try to apply this knowledge to an identification with the character in the play, we must make this transference, this finding of the character within ourselves, through a continuing and overlapping series of substitutions from our own experiences and remembrances, through the use of imaginative extension of realities, and put them in the place of the fiction in the play.

Webster defines substitution as "the act of putting a person or thing in place of another serving the same purpose;

to take the place of." A young actress working on the part of Manuela in *Children in Uniform* was having difficulty with the moment when Fraülein von Bernberg, the teacher she loves and admires, confronts her with her torn chemise and says, "This will never do!" Manuela must react with deep shame and humiliation. The actress could not make this moment meaningful. Neither the garment nor the actress playing the teacher seemed to matter enough to her. Accidentally, I supplied her with a stimulating substitution for both teacher and chemise. I said, "What if Lynn Fontanne had a pair of your soiled panties in her hand and showed them to you?" The actress turned beet red, snatched the chemise from her Fraülein von Bernberg and hid it frantically behind her back.

Many of you are familiar with substitution as it applies technically to an individual moment in a play when the given material fails to stimulate you sufficiently, and you must search for something which will trigger an emotional experience (as in the Manuela incident) and send you into the immediate action of the play. I use the word *substitution* in a much broader sense. In fact, I could even prove that substitution can be used in every moment of the actor's homework and throughout the rehearsal period for every stage of the work. Consequently, it can have its effect on *every* moment of the actor's life on stage. I use substitution in order to "make believe" in its literal sense—to make *me* believe the time, the place, what surrounds me, the conditioning forces, my new character and my relationship to the other characters, in order to send me into the moment-to-moment spontaneous action of my newly selected self on stage.

In putting himself into the circumstances of the play, a talented amateur (as well as a genius actor) often makes substitutions intuitively. If you ask me if it is necessary to make a substitution for something that is already real to you, my answer is NO. If it is real, you have already made the substitution. You tell me you believed it was raining when you looked from your stage window into the wings. Obviously, you took a specific rain (there are numerous types of rain: drizzle, splashy, gentle, torrential, pelting, etc.) that you have experienced in your life and put it into the play at this moment.

An actress told me that Blanche DuBois' young husband was very real to her when she described his death in *Streetcar*, and challenged the necessity of making a substitution for him. It was apparent that she had instinctively made one, otherwise he would have stayed a fiction on the page for her.

At eighteen, when I played Nina in *The Sea Gull* with the Lunts, many elements of the part existed for me in life. Nina is a young, unsophisticated, middle-class girl from the country who is thrown in with a famous actress of whom she is in awe and a famous man (a writer in the play) whom she hero-worships. That *was* my relationship to the Lunts, so I was able to use them head-on.

In *Who's Afraid of Virginia Woolf?* Martha is the daughter of a professor whom she adores; she lives in a college town; and as the play opens, she and her husband are returning from a faculty party. I *am* the daughter of a famous professor whom I adored; I *was* raised in a university town; I *did* attend many faculty parties. Consequently, those things were real to me and directly usable for that particular aspect of my work on the part. However, these moments where an actor's life and the playwright's created life mesh are rare, and so the process of substitution must be thoroughly understood, developed, and practiced until it becomes an ingrained work habit.

Every stage of the search for the part needs endless substitutions from life experience (this includes reading, trips to museums, art galleries, etc.) . Even *bad* films can be of service if the locale has authenticity for you to the point where you can believe you were there. No director can help you with your substitutions since he has not been a part of your life experience. He will help you with the character elements he is after, dictate the place, the surroundings, the given circumstances, and define your relationship to the other characters in the play, but how you make these things real to yourself, how you make them exist is totally private work.

Let me illustrate some of the substitution areas and approximately how you must deal with them (even though I will be dealing with similar problems throughout this book). Suppose I am going to work on the part of Blanche DuBois in *A Streetcar Named Desire*. I have to hunt for an understanding of—and an identification with—the character's main needs: a need for perfection (and always *when* and *how* have I needed these things); a romantic need for beauty; a desire for gentleness, tenderness, delicacy, elegance, decorum; a need to be loved and protected; a strong sensual need; a need for delusion when things go wrong, etc.

If I return to my cliché image of myself—the earthy, frank, gutsy child of nature—I'm in trouble and there will be an enormous distance between Blanche and myself. If, on the other hand, I remember myself preparing for an evening at the opera (bathing and oiling and perfuming my body, soothing my skin, brushing my hair until it shines, artfully applying makeup until the little creases are hidden and my eyes look larger and I feel younger, spending hours over a silky elegant wardrobe, and a day over the meal I will serve before the opera, setting out my freshest linen, my best crystal and polished silver among dainty flowers); if I recall how I weep over a lovely poem by Rilke or Donne or Browning, how my flesh tingles when I hear Schubert chamber music, how tender I feel at a soft twilight, how I respond to someone pulling out a chair for me at the table or opening a car door for me or offering me their arm for a walk in the park—*then* I am beginning to find within myself realities connected with Blanche DuBois' needs.

I was not raised on an elegant plantation like Belle Reve, nor have I lived in Laurel, Mississippi, *but* I have visited elegant mansions in the East, I have seen many photographs of Faulkner country and estates, I have toured some of the South, and from a conglomerate of these experiences I can now make *my* Belle Reve and start to build a reality for my life there before the play's beginning.

Unfortunately, I have never been in New Orleans or the French Quarter, but I have read a great deal, seen many films and newsreels. I have even related the French Quarter of New Orleans, in a way, to a little section of the Left Bank in Paris where I once lived to make it real to myself.

The Kowalski apartment itself, which is dictated for me by the playwright, the designer and the director, must, nevertheless, be made real to me by substitutions from my own life. It is *I* who must make the sense of cramped space, the lack of privacy, the disorder and sleaziness, the empty beer cans and stale cigarette butts, the harsh street noises all move in on me chaotically and frighteningly. Each object or thing that I see or come in contact with must be made particular so that it will serve the new me and bring about the psychological and sensory experiences necessary to animate my actions.

To find a reality for the fatigue, the heat, the oppression, I will have to examine my own life and senses. In *my* relationship to Stella, Stanley, Mitch, their friends and neighbors (as well as to my young husband, my parents and relatives, and the traveling salesman, all of whom *I* talk about but who do not appear in the play), I will have to do a backbreaking job if I am to bring them to a full reality for myself through substitutions and combinations of substitutions.

I never had a sister, nor did I have a relationship with

another girl which was psychologically identical to Blanche's with Stella. I may put together my relationship to a girl who "felt" like a younger sister (of whom I expected respect and attention, whom I enjoyed bossing and giving advice to, and whom I loved) with a relationship to a friend upon whom I felt dependent for love and comfort. I may even use a dozen elements from a dozen different relationships from my past and put them together to build this new relationship with my stage Stella, endowing her at different moments in the play with these borrowed qualities. I must follow an identical procedure with each of the other characters in the play.

Let me emphasize that this process is in flux from the beginning of my homework until the rehearsals have ended. The example of Blanche was given to show you a variety of areas in which you must hunt for substitutions and to give further reasons for the necessity of your understanding this hunt. But there are many more aspects of the work not yet touched upon, which when put together should result in the action for the character, what the character will do. To *do* is a synonym for to *act*. At this point, we are nowhere near the acting; I am still in the process of building a sense of reality and faith in my character.

When an actor has difficulty in finding a substitution for the content of a given scene as a whole, he can usually find the root of the problem in the fact that he's being too literal. Many actors take the outer event and the outer words at face value. For example, the character says, "I hate you" under circumstances where he is actually crying out for attention from someone he loves. But the actor works only for the hate.

Faced with Othello's final scene with Desdemona, an actor may protest, "But how can I find a substitution when I've never had the desire to murder anyone?" Or the Desdemona may complain, "I know I should be terrified, but no one has ever threatened to kill me!" In both instances my answer would be, "I hope not!" But, if at this late stage in the events of the play the actors have not acquired sufficient nourishment to supply a reality for their immediate state of being and consequent needs, they must search for the psychological springboard which will send them into the immediate events. They must hunt out the psychological objective of the scene, and for that they *can* find the substitution.

If I am Desdemona in this scene, I should see that I want to cope with a foreboding of an unspecified disaster. I want to rid myself of a sense of mounting terror. As illogical as it may sound, I can use an experience of waiting in a hospital room prior to surgery, even a dentist's office prior to a tooth extraction. The fears that rush in on me are larger and less static than some fictional, preconceived fear for *a* Desdemona.

If you misunderstand me and again think too literally that during the performance, while lying in a bedroom in Cyprus, you should be imagining yourself in a dentist's office you have skipped the inevitable step of taking this substituted psychological reality and transferring it to the existing circumstances and events in the play: transferring the *essence* of the experience (not the original event) to the scene.

Othello, in turn, should look for the psychological need for retribution, for having to fulfill a great obligation which tortures him and gives him pain. The actor is stopped over and over again by his sense of hunting for a similarity of events in the play and in his own life, rather than a similarity of psychological experiences (for example, the need to punish a child) which then should allow him to accept the events with faith.

Relatively easier to understand and apply are those substitutions used to find a given moment or task in the events which seem insufficiently real (the previously mentioned scene between Manuela and Fraülein von Bernberg). Another kind of example occurred when I was working on the monologue of Mistress Page in *The Merry Wives of Windsor*. She has just received a love letter and gradually realizes it is from Sir John Falstaff, which outrages her. As I was isolating the monologue from the play for an exercise, I had no actor to endow with the necessary realities of my Falstaff. The cliché image of Falstaff with his wide-brimmed hat, puffy red cheeks, mustaches turning upward, pointed beard and bushy eyebrows, and high ruff around his fat neck didn't help me at all. Then I thought, "What if I read this letter and discovered Sidney Greenstreet or Jackie Gleason had written it to me?" Suddenly, the contents of the words in the letter moved in on me strongly and made me laugh, outraged me, amazed me, etc. I had worked with Sidney and knew him personally and adored him, but even if I hadn't, my knowledge of his work in films might have stimulated me similarly, far more than the conventional image of *a* Falstaff.

In *The Country Girl,* there is a point where Bernie Dodd calls Georgie Elgin a "bitch." This should act on me as deeply wounding, insulting, and produce a shocked gasp. But the word itself does not mean much to me. I substituted another word. What if he called me a ". . . ." ? That word does shock and wound me. I imagined that Bernie hurled that word at me, and it drove me up from my chair.

In the same play, there was a moment when my husband, Frank Elgin, betrayed me with a lie and I had to swallow it. My next given action was to take him to the sink in his dressing room and get him a glass of water. I was able to receive the betrayal correctly, but somehow it didn't seem to make the consequent dealing with him specific enough. But what if I thought of myself as a put-upon mother with a naughty child? How would I then deal with my own daughter? The moment I applied this substitution to my Frank, I discovered the *how* of taking his hand, the *how* of almost *pulling* him along with me, the *how* of giving him the glass of water; these actions became specific, in fact, loaded. And I must give special emphasis to the fact that Frank was, at this moment, like a child to me, and something brand new happened between me and the actor. I *no longer* needed to use my daughter. I *had used* her to find *this* reality on stage.

In each example I have made I have also spelled out the action which resulted from the substitution: Manuela grabbed the chemise and hid it; Sidney Greenstreet made me throw and kick Falstaff's letter; my substitution for Bernie Dodd's word made me leap from my chair; my daughter made me pull my husband to the sink. I have *completed* my substitutions by making them synonymous with the actor on stage, the object, the word, the event of my stage life and found a consequent character action. I have used the past to make the present real. I am not playing in the past, but *now.* I have looked for substitutions to believe the now, to feel the now; and done both, in order to find a spontaneous action for now. I will probably repeat this a hundred times because it is so often misunderstood, but your substitutions are complete *only* when they have become synonymous with *this* actor, *this* play's events, *these* objects you are using in your stage life and produce a significant action. You may even forget your original source—*fine!*

I'm certain you have seen an actor on stage with real tears streaming down his face. If your only response was, "Oh, look, real water!" this actor was going to his original substitution, was doing his homework on stage and was failing to connect it to his stage life. Consequently his tears could not move an audience or allow them to have genuine empathy for the character they were observing. To work for an involvement for its own sake on stage bogs down the movement of the play, disconnects you from the play, makes you blind and deaf to the play. Beware.

Substitution

There is still another kind of substitution which I find important in my own work. It is even less literal than those I have already described and less parallel to the character. It is even more personal and private but may be suggestible and stimulating to the actor in addition to his direct life experience. I refer to such intangibles as colors, textures, music, elements of nature. I must admit that I do not know how to teach this, and I assiduously avoid teaching this. I can only make you aware that these "essences" can be valuable sources and warn you to keep them to yourself, as I do myself.

If a new character has, to me, elements of light blue, a field of clover, a Scarlatti sonata, a toy poodle, a shiny blue pond, a piece of cut crystal—these essences may be of value to my sense of self, my particularizations for my character. But if these highly personal concepts are brought out into the open by the director or by me, they always become a hindrance to me. (I have heard a well-known director complain to an actor, "I asked for October tones; you're playing in November tones." What is the actor supposed to do with *that?*) If the director tells me, "I want this character to be like Scarlatti, like a poodle, like a field of clover," I feel swamped by a generality. I question what his statement means to him, and I head straight for general, quality playing, rather than specific character action. I start illustrating a prancing poodle with sharp little Scarlatti-like tones, and I look to the director for approval: "Is it tinkly enough? French enough? Can you smell the clover?" The essence stops functioning for me altogether.

Even the playwright can do a similar thing to you. Tennessee Williams says of Blanche DuBois that there is something about her "that suggests a moth." This image of his blocked me so that I saw myself with fluttering arms on tippytoes banging into a light bulb larger than myself. I had a hard time overcoming it.

43

There is much in a creative process that is almost intangibly real and mysterious—why compound the felony and make it more so?

Please remember that in any example I have given you for substitutions, I was only making my own examples. You must find your own substitutions if they are to be of real value to you. If an example I have made has stirred you, it was an accident, or you simply took mine as a suggestion and found your own—possibly a similar one. *Find your own substitutions*—a warehouse full of them.

And let me warn you of the great trap of sharing your substitutions with *anyone*. Don't fall victim to the temptation of revealing your little goodies to your director or your fellow actors ("Do you know what I'm using here?" etc.). The minute others are in on your source—and they will probably be extremely interested in knowing what it is—they become an audience to your source and evaluate its consequent action accordingly, rather than finding their *own* relationship to the action. You have truly let the cat out of the bag. Your substitution will be gone for you, unusable from then on.

Substitution is *not* an end in itself, not an end to involve you for self-involvement's sake without consequent action. Let me state strongly, in case any of you have misunderstood, that substitution is the aspect of the work which strengthens your faith and your sense of reality in each stage of the total work on character. It is a way of bringing about justified, personal character actions.

Particularizing or to make something particular, as opposed to generalizing or to keep general, is an essential for everything in acting from identification of the character right down to the tiniest physical object you come in contact with.

Substitution

I use the term *particularization* so often that it deserves a little time and space.

I can make an object, a person, a circumstantial fact, etc., particular by examining what is *there* and breaking it down into detail. As a simple example, let me take an ashtray. On occasion, the ashtray given me by the prop man will be, under examination, exactly the sort of ashtray called for in the play. Instead of simply saying, "It's an ashtray sitting on the table in this Greenwich Village garret," I will see that it *is* tin sprayed to look like copper, probably came from the dime store, has two grooves to hold cigarettes, is shiny with a few cigarette stains in the bottom, is lightweight, and I can deal with it correctly under the given circumstances. I have made what is *there* particular rather than just assuming any ashtray.

Now, this same ashtray sits on an elegant marble table in a Park Avenue penthouse. It is supposed to belong there, and from the audience may even pass for elegant. I will make it particular by endowing it with qualities it does not possess by substituting from my previous knowledge of elegant ashtrays. Now, I turn it into real copper, assume it comes from Tiffany, and is heavier than it looks, and would look even better if it were buffed up with polish. I can make it even more particular, if necessary, by finding psychological endowments or substitutions: My husband gave it to me last week for a sentimental occasion. I had wanted it for a long time, and now it sits proudly on my coffee table. Obviously, the simple act of flipping an ash into this ashtray will be influenced by the way in which I have made it particular to me in my character in the play.

Every detail of place, objects, relationships to others, my main character needs, my immediate needs and obstacles must be made particular. Nothing should be allowed to remain general.

4

EMOTIONAL MEMORY

EMOTIONAL memory or emotional recall deals with the problem of finding a substitution in order to release that big burst of tears, the shriek of terror, the fit of laughter, etc., demanded by the playwright, the director or by yourself as interpreter when the given circumstances of an immediate event in the play (something done to you by something or someone) fail to stimulate you sufficiently to bring it about spontaneously. Sometimes the direct substitution (Lynn Fontanne for Fraülein von Bernberg) is not suggestible enough to bring about the desired result. Then the hunt must go deeper in the search for the memory of a big emotional moment.

Occasionally, the term "emotional memory" is interchanged with "sense memory." To me, they are different. I link "emotional memory" with the recall of a *psychological* or emotional response to an event moving in on me which produces sobbing, laughter, screaming, etc. I use the term "sense memory" in dealing with *physiological* sensations (heat, cold, hunger, pains, etc.). Of course, it is true that a physical sensation such as heat or cold can produce emotions such as irritation, depression or anxiety; likewise, an emotional response can be accompanied by or produce physical sensations (such as getting hot or goose-pimply, becoming nauseated).

In life, an emotion occurs when something happens to us which momentarily suspends our reasoning control and we are unable to cope with this event logically. (This is not to be confused with hysteria, a state in which one is flooded by uncontrollable emotions, becomes illogical to the point of losing awareness of and contact with his surroundings and sense of reality, a state to be avoided by the actor at all costs.) At the moment of the release of the control, plus our adjustment to an attempt at control, we are *overcome* by tears, by laughter, or we rage, we bang our fists, or melt with pleasure, to mention only a few results. As pleasurable as the idea of a big emotion may seem to an actor, human beings do not want this loss of control and usually make an attempt to cope with the emotion as it hits them.

If we realize that we did not want this emotion, this loss of control in our real lives at the time when it occurred, we can see how difficult a process it must be for the actor who must now attempt to *recall* the emotion and experience it all over again. This time it is recalled in the service of the play as a genuine revelation of a human being, *not* for any kind of self-indulgence or wallowing about. (If the *character* the actor is portraying is self-indulgent emotionally or caught by hysterics, the actor's selection must still be made to serve the play, not his *own* need.)

To bring about tears, the beginning actor's tendency is to think sad things, to pump for that mood or that general state of being, to try to remember a sad occasion, the story of that occasion, and then pray to God that somehow he will be catapulted into an appropriate emotional response somewhere along the way. I used to make all of these mistakes and could never understand why once in a while, somewhere along the line, something *did* indeed happen to me. But I must emphasize that it happened only once in a while, not inevitably, and it usually took a long time before it occurred. Sometimes I managed to work myself into a near trauma offstage, which brought me on with the sensation of moving in glue. After a few years, I discovered intuitively that what sent me correctly was a tiny remembered object only indirectly connected with the sad event: a polka-dot tie, an ivy leaf on a stucco wall, a smell or sound of sizzling bacon, a grease spot on the upholstery, things as seemingly illogical as those. I used these small objects as stimuli successfully and questioned their logic only in discussion.

Later, I learned from Dr. Jacques Palaci, a close friend trained in psychology, psychiatry and human behavior, that this little indirect object was the *release* object, a release of the censor which moves along with us and says, "Don't lose control." This apparently insignificant object had been unconsciously perceived and associated with the original emotional experience.

To experience for yourself what I am speaking about, tell a friend the story of an unhappy event in your life: tell him, for example, about a time when your lover walked out on you, blaming you unjustly for infidelity. Now tell your friend what surrounded the event; describe everything you can remember about the weather, the pattern of the drapes, a branch brushing against the window, the rumpled collar of your lover's shirt, the smell of the after-shave he was wearing, a frayed corner of the carpet, the tune that was playing on the radio as he left, etc., etc., etc. One of these objects will suddenly release the pain anew and you will weep again.

The consequence of this discovered procedure is endless. You will learn to build your own storehouse of little trigger objects. In rehearsal you will not spend endless time on digging for past *events;* in performance you will avoid "leaving the stage," so to speak, while your mind wanders through a series of past adventures hoping that you will find a specific stimulus. You should have found and filed away many, many specific objects, one of which you will now connect and make synonymous with the event, the person, or the object of your stage life to trigger the response you need.

As for questioning the logic of the object you use from your own experience to take the place of the one you need on stage, let me give an example (especially for the literal-minded student, which, I assure you, is not intended to be facetious). Suppose you are working on Uncle Vanya, and you need a big emotional response for the moment when Uncle Vanya surprises Yelena in the arms of Astrov, a moment when rejection and a sense of loss storm in on him. Suppose then that you have isolated a red apron from an experience in a kitchen when your girl friend's aunt, wearing a red apron, rejected you and turned you out. How do you know that Vanya himself didn't link the moment with Yelena with his *own* red apron, his own sudden recall of a moment of betrayal with his own early rejection? After all, all of our emotional reactions are based on a kind of pile up from our past.

I must warn you, at this point, to avoid the examination of any past experience which you have never talked about or wanted to talk about. Here you will be on dangerous ground because you will not know what can happen to you, and without an understanding or a degree of objectivity to the experience it is useless to you artistically. There are teachers who actually force actors into dealing with something buried (their response to the death of a parent, or the trauma of a bad accident). What results is hysteria or worse, and is, in my opinion, anti-art. We are not pursuing psychotherapy. If you feel mentally sick or disturbed and in need of it, by all means go to a trained doctor or therapist, but *not* to an acting teacher.

When I say that you must have distance from the experience you wish to use as an actor, I am not referring to time, but to understanding. In 1938, I had an experience with the death of someone I loved deeply which I still cannot fully cope with or discuss, and therefore I cannot use as an actress. Yet, I have also had an experience in the morning which I was able to digest and put to use by evening.

Actions themselves, verbal and physical, can generate strong emotions and can sometimes be as stimulating to an emotional release as any remembered inner object. (By inner object I mean an object not outwardly present but an object existing and represented in one's mind only.) The simple act of banging my fist on the table can bring about a feeling of rage. A logical reason or motivation for doing so can load the action for me. Motivated pleading with someone for forgiveness, and sending a verbal or physical action of begging, stroking or clutching may produce a waterfall of tears. The act of tickling someone gently can make me join in a fit of giggles. I don't mean to recommend that you make a practice of predetermining the expression of the action to find the emotion *but* there is a continuous feeding of the action by the sensation or emotion, and the emotion is furthered by the action.

When you claim that an emotion or a recalled object is wearing out for you by repetition, that it has lost freshness, you are failing technically because of a number of possible reasons:

1. You are stopping to demand that you feel, because you have not made your object synonymous with the one on stage.

2. You are anticipating how or at what second the emotion should manifest itself.
3. You have dwelt on the emotion for its own sake, rather than for furthering your stage action.
4. You are weighing the degree of intensity of previous use of the emotional experience.
5. You are fearful that the emotion will elude you, etc. etc.

> Is it not monstrous that this player here
> But in a fiction, in a dream of passion,
> Could force his soul so to his own conceit,
> That from her working all his visage wanned;
> Tears in his eyes, distraction in's aspect,
> A broken voice, and his whole function suiting
> With forms to his conceit?

> [*Hamlet* 2.2. 535–541]

(Conceit means concept here, not vanity, and this is still what it's all about, don't you agree?)

5

SENSE MEMORY

SENSE memory, the recall of physical sensations, is often easier for the actor than the recall of his emotions. If we as actors have any occupational hazards, hypochondria is perhaps one of them. Most of us are interested in our sensations, and examine and discuss them and on occasion make more of them than may be normal for a nonactor. It's all right as long as we remember that these sensations can be usefully expressed. Some actors are so highly sensitized and suggestible that a mere conversation about a pain, a chill or an itch will convince them that they are similarly afflicted. Those actors are the exceptions. Most of us have to learn a correct technique for producing sensations so that they will be readily available to us on stage.

Since the body has an innate sense of truth, we must learn some physiological facts to help us avoid the violation of the physical truth. Sometimes, by a mere incorrect bodily adjustment we can shatter our faith in a whole sequence of our stage existence. It always irritates me when a director or teacher or fellow actor commands me to relax, or concentrate, or use my imagination when my failure in these areas springs from a lack of understanding of the given task. If a playwright or director specifies that I should be sound asleep and then wake up at the play's opening, and I haven't learned what is physically entailed in sleeping or waking up, I will probably lie down and fight for relaxation while, actually, my muscles tense up and my nerves tingle with anxiety. I will fight for concentration as my mind races to inconsequentials because no one has told me on what to concentrate, and my imagination fails me completely in the premise of sleeping or waking because no one has told me down what paths to send it. Even my sensory memory doesn't help unless I were to be allowed an hour or so, and then I might actually fall asleep which, in turn, would not help me to wake up on cue.

It's a relief to discover what the simple physiological process of sleeping and waking entails, and to find out how I can reproduce it in a matter of seconds; how I can execute it quickly, even after running from my dressing room after a quick costume change, jumping into the bed on stage as the curtain rises and the lights come up, and convince myself and the audience that I have been deep asleep and am now waking up. To do this, settle your body snugly into the bed, concentrating on only one area—the shoulders, or the hips, or the feet, for example. Now, close your eyes and center them straight ahead under your eyelids which is the true sleep position (not downward the way they usually are positioned when we first close our eyes). Then direct your inner attention to an abstract object not connected with the given circumstances of the play—a leaf, a cloud, a wave. Now, direct your inner attention from the abstract object to something in the given circumstances—What time is it? Have I overslept? What must I do today? etc. *Then* open your eyes, sit up and pursue your objective. Your eyes will feel heavy, your body slowed down as if after a deep sleep, and by reflex your entire behavior will be influenced for the ensuing activities.

If you are supposed to yawn, you must learn that the physical reason for yawning is a need for oxygen in the brain. Most of you open your mouths wide and *ex*hale, and then jump to another action because it felt so peculiar. Instead, you should *in*hale deeply as you push your jaw down and back *until* the mouth opens, and you continue to pull the air deeply into your lungs before forcing it up into your head as you exhale. You can create a yawn at will in this way so that your eyes may even water.

You can fumble about on stage and believe it is very dark when there's actually enough light for the last row of the balcony to see you, once you understand that when you actually are in the dark your eyes are wide open and the muscles around the eyes are expanded until the eyes feel almost glazed. (I used to think this occurred because I was trying to see better in the dark. Then I realized the converse was true: eye perception was deadened even more by this muscular expansion than by the darkness, but my sense of touch and sense of sound were heightened. Concentration was focused on the feet, the fingers and the ears.) Experiment with this and you will discover that through the one correct adjustment of the eyes you can actually believe that it is dark. Your hands and feet will truly grope for a path through the furniture, and there will be no embarrassing indication of stumbling around.

Bringing about physical sensations for the character's stage life is fraught with many of the same pitfalls as the reproduction of emotional sensations. The actor's tendency is to *think* hot all over, to *think* cold, tired, headachy, sick, and then to wait anxiously for sensations while nothing happens. Or sometimes he waits and is amazed when, by accident, something does happen. If you are supposed to be hot, you must first ask yourself where on your body you are the hottest. Localize one area; for example, under the arms. Remember a sensation of stickiness, of perspiration trickling down, and *then* search for what you do to alleviate this sensation. Raise your arm slightly, see if you can pull your shirt or blouse sleeve away from the underarm to let in a little air. In that moment of adjustment, or attempt to overcome the heat, you will have a sensation of heat. The rest of the body will feel hot, too.

You are to be cold. Do not think cold all over. Localize one area you remember most vividly; for instance, a draft on the back of your neck. Try to recall the sensation and then immediately hunch up your shoulders and stiffen your back a little, even make yourself shiver if you like, and you will have a sensation of cold. (We often shiver on purpose, not only involuntarily, because shivering increases the circulation.) The body will respond to the point where you may end up hopping from foot to foot and rubbing your hands in an effort to get warm (although it might actually be a very warm day).

Fatigue is a condition called for in endless scenes. How often have you seen the entire action dissipated and out of focus because the actor was dragging about and generally trying to feel tired *all over?* There are so many varieties of fatigue. Ask yourself why you are tired, and where. Suppose you have been typing for hours. There is fatigue and tension in your back, across your shoulder blades. Now get up and stretch your back, put your head back and try to relax the shoulder muscles. You will feel exhausted.

Or remember your fatigue on a hot day in August when you walked for hours in thin-soled shoes, and your feet were hot and sore and more tired than the rest of your body. Try to walk gently on your heels to alleviate the soreness and burning under the balls of your feet. Your whole body will follow suit and be accompanied by a strong sensation of tiredness.

I am emphasizing the adjustments to overcoming the sensations because I believe that the sensation occurs most fully at the moment when we are occupied with the attempt to *overcome* it, not when we wait for it while trying only to imagine and remember it. Nor do I mean that you should jump to an outer indication of the adjustment without faith in the cause, or that you should concern yourself with a desire to *show* that you have the sensation. Sometimes you question whether the sensations and consequent adjustments you make will communicate directly enough: Will the audience know that I'm tired?, etc. If on the street you see people without knowing the circumstances of their lives, it may look to you as though the person with a headache is tired, or that the person who has a headache is hot, or that someone with a backache is chilly. However, in a play your conditions are backed up by the playwright and other actors; your headache will be referred to, the heat will be shared by others, the nausea will make you ask for a doctor, etc. The concern for *showing* the condition *must* lead to indication and falseness. It is not your responsibility to show the condition, but to *have* it so you believe it, and deal with it in terms of the play's action.

Even the old cliché of wiping the sweat off the forehead to illustrate heat can become new and valid *if* you stimulate the remembrance of the sweat, the prickling and trickling down from your hairline so that you *need* to wipe it off with the back of your hand.

If you require a cough, find the exact spot in your throat where you remember a tickle or scratch, and you *must* cough to relieve it. If you want a head cold, a stopped-up nose, localize the sense of swelling in the uvula (the soft lobe hanging down at the back of your soft palate) and try to swallow as you contract the uvula. Suddenly, your nose will feel stuffy, and if you blow it you might even produce mucus.

For nausea, pinpoint the queasiness of the stomach, inflate your cheeks slightly, wait for saliva to gather. Breathe deeply and you'll be convinced you feel sick.

For headaches, recall a specific one in a specific spot. For example, directly over the right eye. What kind? Throbbing. What can you do to ease it? Slightly push into it? Rise above it? Pull back out of it? These are tiny adjustments, but after stimulating the imagination to the remembered feeling, they will bring it into the present for you.

For a burn, recall the thin, tight feel of the skin on your fingertip, and how it aches. Then blow on it, flip your hand back and forth to ease it, and you'll be convinced you just burned it.

Sometimes it's only the oozing blood which frightens you when you cut yourself, but remember when it hurts and what you do as you dab the wound with iodine.

Drunkenness, which crops up in countless tragic and comedic scenes, seems to be one of the most difficult to make specific, and traps even fine actors into a series of clichés. Perhaps it is because in this state, with its endless variations from slightly tipsy, to staggering, to thick speech, we have the hardest time remembering. To find it specifically entails the same steps you have used in the search for other physical sensations. First, localize the most suggestive area of your body, give in to it, and then attempt to overcome it. In my case, it is wobbly knees, a loose, weakened condition which I attempt to correct by straightening and strengthening the knees. The other sensations of dizziness, lack of eye-and-manual focus seem to follow. My tongue seems fat and swollen so that I have a wild need to overarticulate. When I am tipsy it usually manifests itself in a psychological need to talk too much, and an assumption that everyone is interested in anything I have to say.

Sometimes you ask, "What if I work for a headache and it stays with me?" I can only answer, "Work for an aspirin." Remember the sensation when the headache eases off, when you hold yourself very still as the tension leaves, and even the back of your neck relaxes as you realize the pain is gone.

This technique—recalling a localized sensation and finding a physical adjustment to alleviate it—is applicable to any condition you may be called upon to play. The accumulation of a lifetime of sensations should be sufficient with our newly acquired technique to serve us for any condition or combination of conditions demanded by the playwright. Even if we are to portray pregnancy or labor and haven't had a baby, or are called upon to have consumption or a heart attack, or to be stabbed to death, or any sensation which, except for having a baby, we hope we won't ever experience, we can still find them within our command if we apply these principles, coupled with a little research on the medical manifestation of the condition. Use the knowledge of substitution to bring bronchitis or pneumonia or a simple chest cold to Camille's consumption; the remembered giddiness from too much cough syrup for a feeling of drunkenness in case you have never had a drink; or the moment when you stayed under water too long and came gasping to the surface as a substitute for strangulation, etc., etc.

To all this, add the magic "If" of imagination to help tie it all up. *If* I were dying! *If* I were in labor!

I trust that you now have sufficient examples to help you find your way for any sensory problem which might arise for you.

Let me warn you of some common errors and misunderstandings in the use of sense memory. The sensations of heat, cold, headache, drunkenness, nausea, and illness, etc., are *conditions* of the scene; rarely is the scene *about* the cold or the headache. The discovery of the sensations and how they influence you is there to condition your actions truthfully in the scene, and with sensory accuracy and faith, but it is not the final aim just to be cold or have that headache on stage.

Furthermore, you are dictating the sensations—they are not dictating you. You will have the sensations to further the actions but not so that they will take over and put you out of control. In line with this, let me state that if a dangerous or unpleasant sensory condition exists for you in your real life, at the same time that your character should have it on stage, avoid it at all costs. If you are really nauseated at the time of having to be nauseated in your stage life, simply avoid the condition or the curtain may have to be rung down. If you really have a headache over your right eye, work for a headache at the back of your head, otherwise the real headache may take over and put you out of control, unable to fulfill your stage life. If you are to be drunk, don't get drunk to be real or the play will turn into something other than the author intended.

In summation, let me state the opinion that a correctly functioning actor should, ideally, be the healthiest, least neurotic creature on earth, since he is putting his emotional and sensory life to use by expressing it for an artistic purpose. If he is employed in the theater, he has an opportunity of making use of his anxieties, hostilities, pent up tenderness through an artistic expression. I think that perhaps the people who call us neurotic or vain or exhibitionistic are unaware how many talented actors are that way only because they are without work opportunities, and therefore release their need for expression in alcohol or unreasonable behavior—or perhaps these people are jealous that when we *do* function we can do what they only dream of doing.

6

THE FIVE SENSES

As a nation we have evidently become so desensitized that encounter groups, an essential part of whose programs seems to be *learning* to touch each other, have sprung up all over the country. The daily hue and cry about an inability of human beings to communicate with each other means that not only do we not reach out to touch, but that we do not contact each other visually or auditorially. Our perceptions are dulled. Full human contact employs all the senses, the more intense they are, the more highly they are developed, the more available is the potential of the actor—his talent. As I have said before, this area of high sensitivity is where true talent lies, and what we make of this sensitivity determines whether or not we can call ourselves artists.

A great danger is to take the five senses for granted. Most people do. Once you become aware that the sources which move in on you when you truly touch, taste, smell, see and hear are endless, you must also realize that self-involvement deadens the senses, and vanity slaughters them until you end up playing alone—and meaninglessly.

There is an amusing story about John Barrymore and the

time he was acting with his brother Lionel, whom he adored. They were supposed to be enemies in the play, and John found it difficult to execute the required actions because whenever he looked into Lionel's soft brown eyes he melted with brotherly affection. It seems that John detested the smell of musk oil, a perfume base, so he secretly sprinkled a little of the oil on his brother's costumes. Whenever Lionel came near him on stage, John was filled with loathing.

I am not recommending this going to an outer reality for help when other substitutions fail, but am simply making an example of the power of smell as a stimulant. A particular odor of leather can send me to a shop on a quaint street in the Tyrol, and I feel the same excitement and romance as when I was there. Think how the scent of cologne or soap can affect you if it comes at you from someone you love. Think how that same scent will affect you by association as it wafts toward you from a casual passerby; how the smell and sound of sizzling bacon can produce a feeling of well-being. An unpleasant smell can be just as suggestive psychologically.

Taste, whether it be of a kiss, or of unpleasant medicine, or something delicious to eat, or strong liquor, is not only important but must be fully explored because in most instances on stage you won't have the real thing, nor will you want it. Liquor should suffice as an example. If your taste buds were alert when you took a slug of bourbon or brandy you will recall what happened to your mouth and throat and stomach. If so, you will be able to endow that slug of colored water on stage with the same properties.

If I have to peel and chop an onion on stage, I will probably use an apple or a potato since the real onion might take over and put me out of control. It won't be difficult to endow the potato with the elements of the onion if I have discovered and been alert to the smell, the consequent congestion in the nose, and the sting in the eyes which makes me cry. Suppose I have to bite into the onion or suck on a lemon. I want a powerful sense of taste so that when I substitute another object for them on stage I will have similar sensations and adjustments.

Explore the endless variations of a simple handshake: if you really make contact, if it is something other than a mechanical, social expression, whether you shake hands with a friend or an enemy, or if it is an introduction to an attractive member of the opposite sex. Alert yourself to the texture of the skin when you make contact with it, the warmth or coolness of the hand, the dryness or dampness, the hardness or softness of the skin, the pressure or the lack of it in the grip.

Start to become more aware of texture, not only of the flesh but of cloth, wood, silver, glass—anything you contact physically, pleasant or otherwise, during the course of your day.

Few people are lucky enough to have all five senses developed with equal intensity, but the actor must hope and pray and work for maximum visual and auditory receiving. The visual contact we make with another human being or with something in nature can act on us like a stroke of lightning if we really open ourselves up to it. If you *really* see a delicate white birch or a giant redwood tree you might weep. If you *really* look at a wave breaking on the shore with the sunlight shining through its crest and its foam, or a black cloud overtaking a little puffy white one, your heart may begin to pound. The same *real* taking-in visually of a human being can produce, "But soft! what light through yonder window breaks? It is the east, and Juliet is the sun!"

The contact our ears make with sound, with words, with melody and tonality are just as crucial to the development and enrichment of our total instrument. To really receive the nuance of verbal action and tone of voice rather than merely factually clicking it off with our auditory sense makes the difference between a fine actor and a hack.

Many of you make some common technical errors in looking and listening. An actor says, "I have such trouble really listening on stage." He is making contact with the individual word that is being sent to him in the mistaken notion that concentration on each word alone will allow him to hear better. Words are sent actively with content. You must listen for the *intent* of the words in order to receive them, giving the words meaning not *only* from their intention, but from your own point of view and expectation.

I don't recommend that you make a rule of this or an excuse for this in your stage life, but in *real* life we don't hear everything that is being said to us. If I propound a long theory on acting and I am *lucky*, you will really hear about three-quarters of it. You will be weighing what you hear against what you already know or think you know, and your attention will often pursue your own paths, formulating the ideas in your own way. Something I have said ten times during a term will arise anew, and an actor's face will light up. "I never heard that before!" His assumptions have changed, and he hears it now in the new framework of understanding. So, on stage, if you particularize the content and intent of what is being sent, and hear *that* under the given circumstances, listening should no longer be a problem for you.

We also "listen" with our eyes. Our eyes, as well as our ears, evaluate and interpret. We interpret content and intention from an expression or movement which the action has given to the words. "You're full of baloney!" sent aggressively with a smirk might infuriate me. The same words sent with a grin and a pat on the back might send me into gales of laughter, depending on who has done what to me.

In the same way that I do not contact the individual,

isolated word while listening, so I do not fasten my eyes to a partner without letting go in order to really receive him while I'm talking. Looking, as well as listening, hinges on needs. Seeing is also balanced against expectations, immediate needs, and your past knowledge of the object.

I sometimes laugh when an actor fixes his partner endlessly during the scene and claims he is working for "eye contact." Try telling someone about an event that just happened to you, and force yourself to keep looking at him while talking. Probably, halfway through your first sentence you will want to look away—not because you don't want to see him, but because while really seeing him you lost contact with the inner objects you were talking about, and so you will forget what you are saying.

Actually, while we talk we look intermittently at the person to whom we're talking in order to see how they react to what we're saying, to see if we have their attention, to see if they get the point, etc. What we see in them at these moments conditions how we continue our tale. In between these moments of eye contact, we contact the inner objects we are dealing with, and our outer, secondary focus is on something inconsequential in the place. Listening and looking are certainly not mechanical processes, but are linked to the center of our psychological and physical being. Simulated looking and listening must produce bad acting.

Because of the enormous importance of the five senses, there should be continuous work on heightening and sharpening them. Anything dormant which you might awaken through daily concentrated attention to your senses will add to your growth as an actor. Unclutter yourselves. Open yourselves up to your fullest capacity—to give meaning to what you *receive* when you see, when you hear, when you taste, when you smell, when you touch.

7

THINKING

You ENTER, stop to flick on the lights, take two steps into the room, and *then* the lights come up. The audience bursts into laughter. Such disasters have happened to us all. If you attempt to verbalize all of the things you *thought* about in the seconds that it took from the flick of the switch to the laughter of the audience, it would probably take you half an hour. Thought moves with such lightning rapidity that any attempt to slow it down is inaccurate, and so must bring about false behavior on stage.

I have often seen an actor sitting on stage, strangely knotted with tension, making faces—furrowing his brow, then smiling, then making a pensive expression. When I ask, "What were you doing?" he answers, "I was thinking." Feeling obligated to illustrate thought, bodily or facially, comes from the mistaken notion that the character's thoughts manifest themselves in an organized progression like dialogue, complete with stage directions like a script. Sometimes the diligent actor mistakenly goes so far as to write out his character's thoughts as if they *were* indeed dialogue. *Real thinking precedes, is accompanied by, and follows action.* Real thinking is active.

THE ACTOR

I sit down, not in order to think, but to rest. I rise to get a glass of water, and walk to my desk to pick up a letter. *While* I sit, rise or walk, I am thinking.

If I put on my coat before going to market, I am not thinking only of my coat unless it is giving me a problem. I am mentally dealing with my grocery list, or with the laundry man, or with a friend who's coming to dinner tonight. My thoughts spring from the contact with these *inner objects* (things or people not present in the room only as images in the mind), and bring about an inner action. Inwardly contacting the grocery list may produce thought about a can of imported French beans and the shelf on which it rests at the supermarket. The beans may lead me to consider how often they are sold out and a possible argument with the manager of the store, or weighing the idea of going to a more expensive store where these beans are more readily available. Contacting the laundryman can produce a remembered event about my last argument with him over the strength of the bleach, and consideration of how I will deal with him today. The friend who is coming to dinner may produce speculation about the new playwright he is bringing with him this evening. In other words, by contacting these inner objects—not present in the room—my thoughts flow forward quickly. Meanwhile the physical task of putting on my coat is completed, having been inadvertently influenced by my thoughts. (I may have yanked at a button when my inner attention went to the laundryman.)

I never ask, "What were you thinking?" Instead, I ask, "What were your inner objects?" so that you will get out of the habit of even verbally analyzing your thought process.

I can accept deliberate thinking only from a philosopher who organizes and arranges the otherwise chaotic and subjective process of human thought into an objective viewpoint of life. He is taking himself out of the action—we actors are involved in it. To act is to do, not to think. The actor's thinking depends on the subjective process of weighing the course of action by a contact with inner and outer objects.

Thoughts and objects which intrude on the concentration on your stage life, those which make for unwanted distractions, most often come from the havoc of your daily private life. (A desire for success can move in on you. Who's out front? An agent? Someone you love? A critic? A rival? Vanity!) All such destructive distractions should be dumped at the stage door before you enter your dressing room. The fight against these intrusions on true thought can be conquered only by strengthening and enlarging the circle of inner objects belonging to the play, and by using them to produce the character's "thinking" in a true life-style.

It must be clear to you now that if any inner object in the play is not real to you, it will have no consequence in producing genuine thought. It will be a dead-end object. Obviously, the thinking process which accompanies the immediate give-and-take with another character on stage, or the thoughts connected to direct action of the play, are easily triggered by the partner, the event itself, and by your sensory awareness. The thoughts are anchored to the events and to the other characters. Not only must these people and events and the things which tangibly surround you be clothed in reality for you by particularization and substitution, but everything that *has* happened, what you *expect* to happen, and what *is* happening connected with the surrounding circumstances as well. The larger your selection of inner objects within these areas, the more food you will have for forward-moving thought and action. Your objects will channel your attention into the private circle of your character's life. You cannot dictate the order of your thoughts or attempt to pigeonhole them in compartments. You must keep them fluid for your character's needs.

8

WALKING AND TALKING

On occasion, I'm certain you have found yourself sitting comfortably in a scene, relaxing into the cushions of the sofa, puffing on a cigarette. You were occupied and involved with another character in the play, and unaware of your body in any sense except that you believed you were there. Then you rose and stood for a while as the conversation continued.

Suddenly, the very act of standing became awkward. You became aware of your hands as unnecessary appendages. Your legs and feet tensed up, you lost a sense of character and place, and you became an exposed actor on stage, not a human being in a room. Then, you protected yourself, attempting to regain composure by assuming a stance—a stage pose. This protective pose was probably borrowed from your earliest and most inept stage experience.

There are many reasons for this kind of physical discomfort and inaccurate adjustment, but the most probable one is that you were gratuitously executing stage *business,* unjustified blocking, following the command, "He rises." You had no relevant justification for the rise or for whatever arrested you in a standing position and this consequently caused you to lose character and orientation to the place. If the rise from the sofa had been connected with the need of the given circumstances (let us say that you rise to get a drink for your friend, to make him feel more at home and welcome, and that on your way to the bar a piece of astounding news has arrested you in a standing position while your attention is riveted to the subject, and that only when the attention waned did you continue to the bar), the standing would be an involving and simple task releasing the body from the sense of being hung up.

Arthur Hopkins, the producer and director, once said, "The reason for walking is destination." Let me add that the movement you create must come from carefully selected action which allows for the organic development of the character and the primary action of the scene.

Even a trap set for us over and over again by the playwright or the director—"He wanders restlessly"—does not have to lead to the usual cliché of mechanical, tense, and general stage wandering. Each movement of true wandering has destination, is focused on a relevant object that we deal with in order to further the character and the story. Suppose that you are alone at home and waiting for a telephone call or a visit from a friend bringing news of a job. You may be impelled to walk to the window to see if he's in sight, and then you may cross to the telephone and consider calling him. You may reject the idea and take it out on the phone by giving it a little push. You cross to the liquor cabinet and actually pick up a glass which you then quickly replace because you have (your character has) a drinking problem. The expected friend is always criticizing your untidiness so you cross to the armchair to rub a grease spot on the upholstery. You cross to a wall mirror and check your hairdo. Meanwhile, your mind races from one inner object to the other—those objects directly connected with your friend, the possibilities of the job, what might stand in its way, etc. In life, your wanderings may seem to lead you to irrelevant objects. On stage, where every second counts, the objects should be selected and dealt with to reveal something new about the character or the circumstances, or both. The *seemingly* illogical objects you have contacted in a strange order must be substantiated by the logic of the play.

You are helped in physical reality by the very clothes you choose to wear. Your psychological state of being, your sense of self, as well as the physical manifestation of it, is strongly influenced by what you wear, even in a simple walk down the street to the corner drugstore to buy a tube of toothpaste. You must make your clothing particular in likes, dislikes, appearance—and with sensory awareness. First assume you are dressed in tight blue jeans, a long Sloppy Joe sweater, and worn sneakers. Now, assume the same destination and identical circumstances of weather, time of day, preceding and upcoming events, only you are wearing a new, classic suit, elegant shoes, fancy kid gloves, and a bright silk scarf around your neck. Then try changing only one thing in the latter example—you think your slightly soiled slip is showing. See how these elements change your entire psychological state of being, and consequently the physical manifestations of a simple walk down the street. (I might take something as small and unimportant as "my slip is showing" for the center of the physicial life of a whole character.)

Clothing so influences my character, is so crucial to me, that I would find it as impossible to come to a rehearsal for Blanche in *A Streetcar Named Desire* dressed in slacks and sneakers as it would be for me to work on *Saint Joan* in a frilly chiffon dress and high-heeled shoes. I could barely get the words out of my mouth sitting around a rehearsal table at a reading.

Of course, the total animation of the body is brought

about by a correct incorporation of surrounding circumstances, weather, time, character needs, relationship to the things and people that surround me, plus main needs and immediate needs. And so is the animation of the words of the character. They are the messenger of my wishes.

The action of the words, how I will send them, for what purpose and to whom, under what circumstances, hinges solely on what I want or need at the moment. This is what must make the words inevitable for my character.

Delivering the words mechanically with set, intellectualized intonations, projecting them beyond the object they are trying to reach and into the audience in the old-fashioned manner, or mumbling without verbal intention or action in the "modern" manner—all come from a misunderstanding of true verbal action. The errors can arise even before rehearsals have begun. The misinformed, diligent actor, if he has time, will sometimes memorize the words and mechanize the inflections before he comes to the first reading of the play. This can be fatal to his final performance. During rehearsals he can hunt for and find intentions for his character, he can attempt to genuinely receive from his partners and his surroundings, and still he will fall back into the identical pattern of the mechanical and rigid "line readings" he had begun with. He can no more change it than he could change arbitrary and unjustified stage blocking which had been arrived at and set for quick convenience. We must learn what our character wants, from whom and under what circumstances, if we are to be propelled into genuine verbal action.

Physical actions are the necessary balance for verbal actions. When the actor is truly alive on stage there is an endless variety of interaction between verbal and physical behavior. Ideally, the audience should be unable to differentiate whether he walks when he is talking or talks when he is walking!

9

IMPROVISATION

Improvisations, which serve for a better understanding of the reality of character, circumstances, time and place, emotions, and the possibilities of varied action, can be of tremendous value. They can even bear fruit in the creation of the physical and verbal life of an entire play (not conceived by a playwright), as exemplified so beautifully in the Story Theater of Paul Sills.

Improvisational techniques could fill a separate book. I will only enumerate those techniques which are useful to the actor in a written play in the chapter entitled, "The Rehearsal." I'm sure we agree that acting is the response to an assumption by doing something to somebody at a given place and time in order to bring about human behavior which can be seen and heard by an audience. Therefore, the value of improvisational exercises away from concrete sequences of the play to find spontaneous actions and emotions must become obvious.

Improvisations of a kind are continuously taking place, whether we are creatively testing the text by reading it, or are on our feet opening up an imaginative playground. Everything and anything can be improvised, and some of the findings will be of service for a given play. We should be guided by the game of make-believe which we played so well when we were children.

Avoid general ad-libbing, set up time and place and objectives and who you are. Surprise each other as partners. Don't paraphrase. Use the magic "If" in endless variations, and you might come up with gold.

10

REALITY

"I CAN'T BELIEVE IT!" "This isn't real!" How often do we say this about an overpoweringly real event in life? We are balancing the experience against the daily, ordinary manifestations of life. Christopher Fry once said: *"Reality is incredible,* reality is a whirlwind. What we call reality is a false god, the dull eye of custom."*

We have to open all our senses and innermost feelings to the *extra*ordinary realities of existence. We have to receive these realities with innocence and freshness, as though we had just been born. To create, one has to take known elements and make something new of them, and as we have only a few hours of compressed life on stage, our creation better count. We must *take* from life, and *what* we take must have pertinence. A mere imitation of nature in its familiar, daily aspects is the antithesis of art.

In the preceding chapters, I have not yet differentiated between truth in life and truth on stage. I have continuously stressed life realities (and will continue to do so) in an effort

* "How Lost, How Amazed, How Miraculous We Are," *Theatre Arts,* August 1952.

to steer away from the misconceptions and customs of old theater conventions, false theatricality, tricks and gimmicks. But truth in life as it is, is not truth on stage. If I bring real snow into the theater it will melt, even before the curtain goes up. I remember a play in which real milk boiled over on cue on the stage stove. The audience was *dis*illusioned as they audibly speculated on how this had been mechanically achieved. In *Look Back in Anger,* Mary Ure ironed with a real steam iron. Not only did the audience murmur, "Real steam!" as they missed what she was saying, but at one performance she was scalded, and the curtain was rung down.

There is a lovely story about the old German actor Albert Basserman during rehearsals for a play in which it was supposed to rain. The director and the designer were worrying about real water and how it could be produced on stage. Basserman interrupted them: "When I come on stage, it rains!" And everything in his behavior convinced you that it *did!*

I once played with an actor who had to take me by the arms to shake me. After showing him that I had to put more makeup on my bruised arms than on my face, he apologized with, "I'm sorry, but I really felt it!" and promptly went on stage and bruised me again. Finally, at one performance I screamed as he dug his fingers into the muscles of my arms. He forgot his lines and let go of me in wild confusion. Backstage he confronted me: "You weren't supposed to scream there." I explained, "I'm sorry, but I really felt it." He never hurt me again.

It is not "real" simply to slug it out in a stage fight and possibly send an actor into the orchestra pit or to the hospital. Really hurting someone is like the boiling milk: the audience concerns itself with the wounded actor instead of with the character he is portraying. To bring about a "real" fight requires the detailed and controlled definition of each

THE ACTOR

movement. The physical action must be as concrete as the words of the playwright.

The intruding realities which spring from our private lives must be put aside so that our stage realities will be allowed to evolve spontaneously. If my Romeo has garlic on his breath it is unreal to the play. It is also unreal if I "use it" as is. (So many actors employ this phrase, evidently meaning that *whatever* moves in on them on stage is supposed to be spontaneously put to use.) In *Romeo and Juliet,* garlic is not a part of Shakespeare's dictum. I can plead with the actor after the performance not to eat garlic again, and if this fails, try to ignore it or desperately endow it with attar of roses.

To swat at a live roach on stage in a room that should be a palace may not only be irrelevant to the play and the character, but will take the audience away from the truth of the stage life. You must see what you *have* to see in order to tell the story, or see it so that it doesn't distort the story.

To go from the ridiculous to the sublime, I would like to cite the example of Jean Louis Barrault's Hamlet, in the scene of his advice to the players. While the chief player was emotionally reciting about Hecuba, Hamlet quietly approached him and literally lifted a teardrop from his cheek, balancing it on two fingers and regarding it in wonder. It later catapulted him into, "Is it not monstrous that this player here . . ." etc. This is an example of poetic action which might never occur in life, but which became *real* and deeply meaningful on stage because Barrault really did it and believed it so that we in the audience did, too.

In our search for genuine emotion and sensation and truthful behavior and action, we should never forget that selection is our goal. Nor should we forget the obligation to the playwright. We can perhaps aim to give him even more than he had hoped for by our revelation of the detail of the human being he envisaged.

Reality

In defining the difference between reality in life and reality in art, Tolstoy said, "Something is added to nature which wasn't there before." That "something" is the artist's point of view and his power of selection, which comes *from* life and makes for *new* life.

PART
TWO

THE OBJECT
EXERCISES

INTRODUCTION

A performing musician, a singer or a dancer is extremely fortunate in that he is presented with specific exercises from the time he decides to pursue his chosen art form. He is forced into certain disciplines and consequently learns to develop them. He must use them daily, and they stay with him until the end of his career. He can practice them at home and put in as many hours a day as he chooses, to perfect his abilities.

As an actress, I have always envied these artists. I can participate in some of their disciplines. I can study dance, and practice my stretches and pliés alone. I can study voice and speech, and practice my exercises alone. I can study an instrument and enlarge my musical sense. I can read and study literature, history and plays, and know that I am enlarging my understanding of the theater. I can work on roles to a certain extent, and I can work on monologues. But in the area of human behavior, its discovery and enlargement, I usually have to wait for a part and rehearsals with my fellow actors. This always frustrated me as an actress, and so I began to devise exercises for myself to tackle a variety of technical *problems that continued to bother me. Now I present these ten* Object Exercises *to you.*

Let us take the problem of trying to find and re-create two ordinary minutes out of life when alone—two minutes when I say I wasn't doing anything (impossible!), when nothing happened. To say this is akin to saying that nothing happens in Chekhov, to which I have heard the retort, "Nothing does happen except that one world comes to an end and another begins."

What are the components of two consecutive minutes of my life—not in crisis, but in the pursuit of a simple need? What do I have to know if I want to re-create those two minutes of existence?

Who am I?	Character.
What time is it?	Century, year, season, day, minute.
Where am I?	Country, city, neighborhood, house, room, area of room.
What surrounds me?	Animate and inanimate objects.
What are the given circumstances?	Past, present, future, and the events.
What is my relationship?	Relation to total events, other characters, and to things.
What do I want?	Character, main and immediate objectives.
What's in my way?	Obstacles.
What do I do to get what I want?	The action: physical, verbal.

These are the questions we must ask ourselves, and explore and define in order to act. For the time being, I would like to free you from the interpretative problems of a given play and a character, and ask you to apply these questions to a simple exercise of finding and re-creating two minutes out of your own life when you were alone.

EXAMPLE: I am sitting at this typewriter writing this chapter.

Who am I?	I have a strong, still too narrow, sense of identity and self-image formed by my parents, my origins, education, sociological influences, loved ones and enemies—all the things a human being is conscious of.
What time is it?	10 A.M. on September 12, 1972. We're in the middle of presidential campaigns. Vietnam bombing raids are on the morning news. The air is very still. The light from outside has a slightly hazy glare. I am sitting in a sunsuit because it is quite warm.
Where am I?	My house in Montauk. I am working at the white Formica table in the dining area off the living room. The kitchen is to my left. Through the window to my right I can see the sundeck, and beyond it the grassy dunes topped by the shell of a World War II lookout tower, long abandoned. Behind me the sun is pouring through the living room.
What surrounds me?	The typewriter is new. House plants, which I recently watered, are in the corner. The white tabletop reflects

brightly. In the kitchen a fly is buzzing over the newly washed breakfast dishes. My poisonous cigarettes are at my elbow, and the ashtray needs emptying. My poodles bark at a passing car. My notes lie piled up in disorder behind the typewriter.

What are the given circumstances?

My collaborator on this book is expected. We have been working all summer. I have been procrastinating since 7 A.M. by cooking, cleaning, arranging flowers, watering the grass, arranging unanswered mail and all my notes on "The Object Exercises." My book is years in the making. A deadline is coming up.

What is my relationship?

To the book: it represents the expression of my work both as a teacher and as an actress.

To Haskel: he is my collaborator, and also my house guest during the writing of this book.

What do I want?

To be of service, to be a participant in society as well as to be needed by those I love. To be a part of art and nature. To live up to responsibilities. (*Main Objective*) —To finish this chapter.

(*Immediate Objective*) —To have a few pages to show him when he arrives at noon.

What's in my way?	Time: he's coming in two hours. Weather: its gorgeous outside. The garden: the vegetables need to be weeded. I would enjoy a frothy, cold drink. I'm unclear about the organization of the chapter. The onionskin paper crinkles in the typewriter. My poor typing skill, and many typos.
What do I do to get what I want?	I type. I make typos. I race ahead. I light a cigarette after emptying the ashtray. I battle with content. I battle with order. I take a breather outdoors, and sniff the clematis. I yell at the poodles. I write ten sentences with clarity. I deserve a drink.

These areas are the essentials to examine in order to define what makes this moment in my life evolve. Every one of them and many more influence and make this moment inevitable. The examples I have made in each area are minimal to finding my behavior for the moment. Some of the things are primary and deal with the conscious execution of the task, and some are secondary.

In turning this examination of a few minutes of your life alone into a practical exercise, I ask you not only to test all aspects mentioned above but to pinpoint all of the physical and psychological sensations inherent in them, and then to make a layout of the action for the two minutes you have examined. Then see if you can re-create them as if for the first time.

I have given an example of something I was doing now at this moment of writing. I could take a remembered event from last *year, or season or week. I might select the same objective (to finish a chapter) and put it at a different time (March 11, two years before in Greenwich Village on a raw, sleety day, with knocking radiators in an untidy apartment. The garbage men are on strike. I might have a head cold, be wearing an old bathrobe and terry-cloth scuffs. A marred leather-top desk, my twenty-year-old Remington typewriter. hot tea at my elbow, some Vicks cough drops and Kleenex, the telephone ringing incessantly, unwanted company coming for dinner at night, etc.—and I will discover different behavior and actions.*

Object exercises should not be improvisations, although a degree of the rehearsal process will obviously involve them. But the final work should be exactly like that on a scene or a play, and you should be able to repeat a precisely defined concept broken down into actable elements (comparable to the score of a musician), as if it were happening for the first time. The only difference between the exercise and a scene is that you will be using yourself instead of a character, and your life experience instead of a play. The addition of the play requires that you find yourself in a character, using the auditory and visual concept of the playwright, director and designer.

You will work on these exercises by yourself under circumstances when you find yourself alone. This will also help you to develop discipline, which most actors are so sadly lacking—the discipline to work and to explore all by yourself. (No partner to tell you, "Let's get down to work.") Step 2 will be the testing of your exercise in communication with your teacher and peers. The final work, when you apply the problems of any exercise to a play, will, of course, include the powerful recognition not only of the writer but of the other actors.

When you first work on the exercises you will probably

balk for all of the reasons I mentioned in dealing with "Identity." You will think you are boring, and you would rather look for eccentric circumstances or "interesting" events. Remember the cat!

Don't become bad playwrights. What should compel you into actions are definite needs, not show-off inventions. Don't look for melodrama or eccentric tales, no eviction notices, suicide notes or tragic love affairs. An actor once brought in an exercise in which he prayed to God in a cathedral, ran behind the curtain, fired several shots, staggered back on stage, and died in front of the Madonna. Don't look for a B-movie story, but a discovery of your behavior under simple circumstances when fulfilling a precise need. To convince a group of your colleagues that you are alive *with forward-moving action for two minutes—that this never happened before in spite of the preciseness and detail of your selections—is what you should aim for. If you can convincingly create two minutes on stage in which you exist as if you were alone at home, you will have succeeded.*

The very fact that you have no playwright's interpretation to hide behind ("But the character *would feel, he would do, or wouldn't do . . .") forces you to examine all sources and behavior with no excuses. You also are establishing habits of self-exploration which later can be put to use for character. Furthermore, you will establish the habit of working in many of the areas you must use in a scene. The exercise will help you to test selection and pertinence.*

After having rehearsed and devised the exercises, the problem of presentation—how and where—will be an individual one. If you are a professional actor, you will undoubtedly have a studio or workshop available, with sufficient space, equipped with basic furniture and props (a bench or sofa, a bed, a bureau or desk, a cabinet that can do for a refrigerator, tables—one of which can substitute for a stove or sink—chairs, a blanket, some cushions or pillows, books, bottles, magazines, ashtrays, etc.). If you are lucky, there will be a movable flat or two with workable doors, and perhaps even a window. You will present your scenes to a teacher or your peers for criticism and possible reworking.

If you are an aspiring actor, you should find a qualified teacher who will provide you with the same physical setup, and if you are a teacher interested in testing these exercises you should provide all of the above for the students.

Necessary personal objects which you know can't be supplied, like clothing or an iron or a particular dish, pot, glass or book, must be brought by the actor. As a matter of fact, people who know me will recognize anyone studying with me as they approach the Studio, because they are usually lugging so many shopping bags full of props.

Since place is crucial, let me remind you that when you examine every aspect of it at home to see what influence it plays on your life, already begin to make considerations for how it can be transferred and constructed elsewhere. Use real objects. These are not pantomime exercises. Avoid any task that will force you to pantomime an activity with an incomplete object (like opening or closing doors when there are no doors to work with). Take what's there and, if necessary, endow it physically and psychologically with what it should be.

The exercises are not mute. If you find that you grunt, use expletives, or verbalize when alone, fine. It will help you with later exercises.

A minimum of one hour of rehearsal for each two-minute exercise is recommended—and by rehearsal I mean doing it, not just thinking about it.

Testing the communication of your selected existence

with your "audience" is, of course, the proof of the pudding
in the value these exercises will have for you.

THE TEN OBJECT EXERCISES

1. *The Basic Object Exercise*	Re-creating behavior which leads to the achievement of a simple objective
2. *Three Entrances*	Preparation and its influence on the entrance
3. *Immediacy*	Dealing with the problems of anticipation while searching for something lost or mislaid
4. *The Fourth Wall*	The guarantee of privacy while using, not ignoring, the visual area of the audience
5. *Endowment*	Dealing with objects which cannot have total reality because they might otherwise totally control you; heightened reality
6. *Talking to Yourself*	The problem of the monologue
7. *Outdoors*	a) Relationship to space and nature b) Finding forward-moving occupation without the help of furniture and props
8. *Conditioning Forces*	Learning to put together three or more sensory influences—heat, cold, physical pains, hurry, dark, quiet, etc.

THE OBJECT EXERCISES

(The last two exercises employ a character from a play)

9. *History*   Identifying with and finding realities of historic time and place (the character taken out of crisis in the play)

10. *Character Action*   Objects as they affect two different characters in terms of behavior

11

THE BASIC OBJECT
EXERCISE

THE BASIC object exercise places no emphasis on any particular technical problem. It simply should test your ability to re-create two minutes of your life and bring it to presentation as if for the first time.

Incorporate all the questions on page 82 except perhaps the first, since I assume you *know* who you are—or think you know. First, give yourself an event or a simple task and establish your circumstances—past, present and future.

For example, you are coming home exhausted and want to make yourself comfortable. I have suggested your "home" for the place of your exercise so that you will explore all of the things in your surroundings that continuously influence you when you are alone, which, until now, you have probably taken for granted. And don't ignore the influence of the city and neighborhood of your living quarters.

If you are uncomfortable you must ask yourself, What is uncomfortable—and why? Suppose your feet hurt. Why? You walked the "rounds" of producers' and agents' offices on a hot, sticky day in July. You were wearing thin-soled sandals which rubbed at the back of your heels. You were rejected by agents in a variety of ways—coolly and courteously told, "Nothing today"; rudely and humiliatingly told, "You're too fat for the part"; offhandedly informed, "Try us again next week." The producers were away on vacation.

You have just climbed three long flights of stairs and had trouble locating your key, and you come into your apartment to flop, only to find a disorderly apartment. Now you pursue your objective to try to get comfortable. You drop your portfolio with its photos and credits on the table. Painfully, you remove your sandals and leave them near the door. You go to the window to open it further for more air. Soot from the windowsill blows in and dirties your hands. You hobble to the sink to wash your hands, etc., etc. You end up sitting at the kitchen table soaking your feet in a bowl of warm water while you cry softly into your vodka-and-tonic, feeling sorry for yourself. You are comfortable!

OR

TIME: 7:10 on a beautiful spring morning in 1973.

PLACE: In your bed on Perry Street in New York City.

SURROUNDINGS: Your alarm clock is on the antique night table at the right of the bed. The window is wide open; the white Orlon curtains are blowing, and the early light is shimmering. The streets are still except for isolated foot-steps and barking—someone is walking a dog. Your chiffon robe is across the room on a stiff, white chair. One slipper is next to the bed, the other was kicked under it, etc.

GIVEN CIRCUMSTANCES: *Past*—You had a heavy date last night and went to a great new French movie. You had a little too much to drink and showed off. You slept heavily and got the bed clothes tangled. You slept ten minutes past the alarm.

Present—You are considering how to stay in bed a little longer. You see a man in an apartment across the street

92

watching you in bed. You wonder how to get to your robe and slippers.

Future—You have a reading for a part in a play today. You have another meeting with last night's date later on.

RELATIONSHIP: To your date—possibly serious for the future; tender, humorous. To the young director of the new play you're going to read for—he thinks you're terrific and right for the part, but isn't sure he can persuade the producer. You've worked for the director in stock and "handle" him easily. To the peeping Tom—he's done this before, and you'll give him his money's worth. You love your new robe, earned from a commercial. The slippers are tacky and should be thrown away. Your date's cigarette butts have a musty, stale smell in the ashtray on your bureau.

MAIN OBJECTIVE: To prepare for the reading.

IMMEDIATE OBJECTIVES: To get your robe and slippers on. To get a cup of coffee and some juice. To get the script ready with pencil and pad in order to study the scene you will prepare. To lay out a proper wardrobe for the audition and to make yourself elegant.

OBSTACLES: Time—you have only until ten o'clock before the reading. Physical—you're slightly headachy from the extra drink. Weather— it seems too balmy and beautiful to work. The script is badly Xeroxed and difficult to decipher. The peeping Tom won't leave his window, etc.

ACTIONS: You leap out of bed and flaunt your behind in your thin nightie at the peeping Tom, before yanking the curtains together and putting on your gorgeous robe. You turn the clock to the wall so that your lateness won't rattle you. You empty your friend's ashtray in the attempt to get him off your mind. You look for an aspirin for your headache, etc., etc.

These examples should stimulate ideas for an approach to your own basic object exercise. The order of examination of the various categories is not as important as the fact that you eventually cover them all. You may begin with a relationship to someone and build an objective around that, which you then clothe in circumstances, or you may begin with an objective. Let me repeat that no matter how much you improvise in the course of your rehearsals, the final work entails the decisiveness of the actions which have evolved from your particularizations of all the elements I have described in such detail. I sometimes call this your final score. The final shape you give the whole, the determination of the objectives, whether they succeed or fail as they lead you on to the next one should become inevitable. And your craft will be tested by your ability to present the final shape with the spontaneity of the first time.

How much of your behavior has been subconscious and reflex will become clear to you as you put it under the microscope in this fashion. You should also discover that your actions are dependent on your wishes and the objects which surround you.

All technical variations of the ensuing exercises incorporate the elements you have examined in this one. Don't omit any of them.

12

THREE ENTRANCES

HAVEN'T you stood nervously in the wings waiting to make an entrance, fighting for concentration to gain faith in your character, in your circumstances, in your very state of being, while stagehands scurried around, whispering near the light board, and other actors chatted distractingly? If you were *on* stage when the curtain went up, although some of the distractions were similar, at least you were surrounded by furniture and objects which allowed you some kind of illusion. You didn't stand frozen while waiting for the curtain, but probably connected yourself with some small doing which came from the events that would lead you forward into your activities as the curtain rose.

How to overcome the ice-cold shower-shock of the first contact with the audience as "He enters" from backstage onto the stage has been a problem for even some of the great stars I've worked with. Actors protect themselves from this shock usually in one of two ways, both incorrect. In the extreme, they either sneak on and into the stage area, floating inconspicuously without decisive action until some object engages them so that it must really be dealt with, or they smash on stage with an attitude of accept-me-or-else-dammit until their involvement with a task becomes genuine. In the wings, they either review all of their homework—background, circumstances, relationships, events, substitutions—until the brain is gummed up and the thinking diffused, or they think of themselves as a "pro" who doesn't need "all that stuff," and whisper jokes to the nearest stagehand just before they enter. Either way spells disaster.

After many years of playing, of trial and error, of faulty entrances, and of wondering why in performance maybe three out of eight first entrances in a week were successful, I was finally able to distill from the successes three essential steps of preparation. Anything *more* or *less* left a gap or interfered with my goal: to come *into* my stage life *from* a past as if for the first time with the full involvement of my character, with purpose, in focus. In other words, I want to be *in,* not *on!*

Assuming that I have shed my private problems and my private address long ago at the stage door, and that I have slowly and calmly applied my makeup and dressed my character (and started to put my attention toward my character's life while doing it), and assuming that the rehearsals and homework were thorough and complete, what can I do backstage while waiting for my cue? First of all, I must convince myself with true innocence that I exist *now*—not yesterday. I cannot think that I will repeat my last performance or my last rehearsal, yet I have to trust that whatever I found in them will serve me now. Spontaneity, a feeling of immediacy, can only be achieved if I give my whole attention to this moment. My three essential steps of preparation are: What did I *just* do? What am I doing right *now?* What's the first thing I want?

And then, go for it! Even after I discovered that these three steps worked for me, I occasionally muddied an entrance or left room for anxiety and tension by simply paying lip service to the steps or mechanically clicking them off. They must be fully done!

This object exercise involves the preparation for, and the making of, an entrance utilizing the three steps just mentioned. Having settled on the circumstances, time, place and objectives of your exercise, vary and make changes in steps 1 and 2 to see how they influence and change step 3.

EXAMPLES: An early morning in late November. You slept seven hours with a minimum of anxiety dreams. You are in the middle of rehearsals on a workshop production. You are facing an interesting problem with your "big" scene in the rehearsal ahead of you today, and you want to be at your very best for it. After having gotten up from your bed, your first objective is to get a cup of coffee to clear your brain.

Step 1 (*offstage*) You give your attention to the fluffy new bedroom slippers you have *just* put on.

Step 2 You are standing outside your kitchen door while you actually *are* yanking at the belt of your robe, pulling it too tightly around your waist because you've gained a pound.

Step 3 You open the kitchen door and look to see if the coffee pot is on the side of the sink, washed and ready. It is. You head briskly toward it: your taste buds are primed for the coffee. You have *entered* without knowing it, in the pursuit of your wishes.

Then change it

1. You have *just* stubbed your toe on the edge of the bed.
2. You stop outside the kitchen door and *are* rubbing your toe, which makes you remember a comic toe-stubbing routine that breaks you up.

3. You come into the kitchen and discover the coffee pot on the stove, so you blissfully hobble toward it to re-heat the coffee you made freshly last night. (You have *entered* laughing.)

Then change it

1. You give your attention to the assumption that you have *just* brushed your teeth.
2. You *are* tasting the toothpaste, running your tongue across your teeth and considering an overdue dentist's appointment.
3. You *have come into* your kitchen to hunt for the coffee pot which is ready on the table. You quickly fill the pot with water, singing loudly to push the idea of the dentist out of your head.

Or take circumstances such as coming home on a crisp October day at three in the afternoon from shopping in order to prepare a gourmet dinner for six people. Your groceries are being delivered immediately. You are outside your front door, and the telephone is ringing in your apartment. You hope it isn't one of the guests reneging on your invitation.

1. The superintendent *just* shouted that your rent is over-due.
2. You *are* getting your key out.
3. You unlock the door and run to the phone before it stops ringing.

Then

1. You *just* took off your coat as you ran up the last flight of stairs.
2. You *are* picking up your keys which fell from your coat pocket.

3. You frantically get the door open and *throw* your coat on the floor because the phone has stopped ringing.

Then

1. You *just* saw a roach on the welcome mat.
2. You *are* using the wrong key in the door.
3. You finally *get* the door open and shiver in disgust as you *sidle* to the phone, looking for more roaches en route.

In each instance, you have set yourself the task of a continuance of your life, which has brought you from the past into the present with a future at stake, as opposed to the task of "entering" or simply getting on stage. While waiting for the entrance, you have responded to an imagined immediately preceding event by a real doing which allows you to continue your assumed life on stage. The examples for the entrance are primitive; nevertheless, to begin with, choose equally primitive ones.

Later, when they are applied to scene work or to the individual entrances of a character in a play, there are, of course, many other principles at stake:

1. No matter how precisely you have selected your off-stage stimuli and consequent doings, they will have little or no value unless they feed and act as a springboard for the life which must be fulfilled on stage. You must be tuned in to the experience of your character.

2. Your selections must be in harmony with the character's state of being, whether it is at a depth of despair or peak of emotional crisis or at peace with the world. (Refer back to Chapter 4, "Emotional Memory.")

3. Whatever preparation you used to *lead up* to these immediate three steps before the entrance is highly personal and can take many forms. Reexamine what has served you in

the past, if you are an experienced actor, and see what can serve you now. If you are inexperienced, you will experiment with many things. Quiet, stillness, aloneness always help me to clear the way. Empty yourself like a vessel so that you can fill yourself with your character. I like to compare myself to an athlete who must warm up for an event. Victory is not a result of panting and puffing and tensing up.

4. If the scene itself is muddy or ill-defined, the entrance may be of only momentary service, or, more likely, it will be chosen for its own sake rather than as an essential beginning for the total scene.

5. There is an added dimension to the entrance—one so highly individual that it is difficult to make theoretical, yet it should be mentioned. An actor playing a fight manager making an entrance into his fighter's changing room used the three specific steps to bring him from the outdoors into the room, but still somehow he felt it wasn't enough; he wanted something more for his character. He himself wasn't as muscular, powerful, and aggressive as the role required. He solved his problem by imagining he had just walked against a strong gale. It actually transformed him as he entered.

The exercise for an entrance can go beyond just the problem of preparation in its usefulness by making you examine the endless variations and small adjustments you have to choose from, after which you must test how they can change an entrance, and from these changes prove to you how important the final selection should be to serve a character in a play. By repetition and correct execution, when you present this exercise you will see that you have dealt with the essentials for involvement and immediacy, which leaves no room for entrance "nerves."

When making an entrance in a play, you must come in with the expectancy of the character's life, and encounter what actually moves in on you—with the problems your character meets with which compel you to fulfill your character's needs through the character's actions!

I will never forget the magic created by Laurette Taylor's first entrance in *Outward Bound*. She came onto the stage *backwards,* stepping over the high sill from the deck to the salon of the boat, still nodding and bidding farewell to an imagined passenger on the outer deck. Once into the salon, she turned to the people on the stage, and recognized her son with a wailing, "Owwww!" Did that entrance ever come from a past into the present with a future!

13

IMMEDIACY

THE FIGHT to prevent anticipation, to prevent thinking and planning ahead, to prevent setting yourself for an action already knowing what its consequence will be, and how to arrive at immediacy (It is happening *now*) is a struggle that seems to go on and on, for established actors as well as for those just beginning. We know that we shouldn't anticipate. We know that when we do, our actions become mechanical, and we start to concern ourselves with the outer form, and bad acting always results. We even *know* that we *should* give ourselves with innocence and trust to the moment and allow it to evolve into the next.

In life we think ahead and have expectations about what will happen but even when, on occasion, we are right, we never know *how* it is going to happen. And, of course, we never know if we will succeed or fail in fulfilling these needs. We have future plans of action and think ahead to the other possibilities when the one we are involved with is unsuccessful or tedious. It goes without saying that this is an entirely different process from the one of anticipating our character's actions or the actions which are directed to us.

In order to isolate the problem of anticipation and search for the immediacy of a moment, and go from theory to practice, I suggest an exercise in which you will test immediacy by hunting for something you have lost or mislaid. Misplacing or losing something is an almost daily occurrence. Become aware of what you do and what happens to you. Find the human logic behind what may seem outwardly illogical in the stages of your hunt. (I have looked for a purse under a single sheet of paper on occasion.)

I don't mean that you should select only irrational or idiotic behavior, but if you discover it, don't eliminate it from your score but give it human *cause*. After a few days of self-observation you will probably get ideas for the exercise—the circumstances under which you would look for a given object or a lost one. Give yourself high stakes in this object—a treasured earring or watch, a love letter, money. Even a lost comb can have importance if your hair is a mess, and you are on your way to an audition and have no brush.

Do not preconceive or shape the psychological or emotional effect of your inability to find it, or the moment of discovery. Most of you have the mistaken idea that the emotions rise upward and increase on an even curve until they reach a peak. On the contrary, our anxieties, frustrations, disappointments, angers and joys may be charted like the fever of a patient when his temperature jumps up, drops down, levels off, drops and climbs again. Leave room in your work for this. If a sudden calm settles over you, don't judge it as wrong for your circumstances—it may precede the storm.

You are on your way out to an important engagement, putting on your gloves as a finishing touch. You check your bag for your house key. It's not in your bag where it ought to be. You know that you will be returning late, and the superintendent will be asleep, unable to let you in. Your roommate is away for the weekend, you won't be able to get back into your apartment without your key. You empty your bag and look through the contents. You replace them. You check your pockets. You look other places where the key ought to be, where it might be, where it ever was, and if all else fails, where it couldn't possibly be. You methodically rifle your bureau drawer, run to your closet, grab your raincoat, put your hand in the pocket, and the key is found.

After improvising on your circumstances until you have found many possibilities for objects to deal with in the hunt, places to search through, and the endless variations of behavior which result, make precise decisions about your course of action and give cause to it, as well as to your expectancies. If your plan remains too loose, you will still be improvising when you present the exercise, and you will only be testing the technical problem of anticipation at a minimum.

Anticipation does not present itself as a problem only at the moment of finding the lost object (which you yourself have concealed) but at every moment of the search. Go through the bag where you expect your key ought to be with faith and conviction; *really* examine the contents until you are certain it isn't there. *Really* look into the bureau drawer and *know* that it might be there, because it has been on several occasions. Go to the next logical or possible place with the faith that you might have left it there and *really* give your full attention to it so that, if anything, your need to find the key will strengthen. The expectancy and speculation as to where it could be or should be, the trying to remember where it was last or where it was yesterday, is inherent in every search.

If the exercise succeeds for you, a genuine sensation of relief or joy or perhaps rage will come over you when you finally put your fingers on the key in the corner of your raincoat pocket. And this process of genuinely getting caught up in each moment can reoccur while you are following a specific plan which you may have repeated for the tenth—no, the hundredth—time.

A few mechanical problems should be considered which haven't arisen before in the other exercises. In order to keep your faith high, you must take even more care in reconstructing the place. Be sure that you have enough places to look. If at home you looked through drawers which were crammed with belongings, make sure that the drawers in your studio have makeshift things in them. Nothing will break your faith more quickly than yanking open an empty drawer and having to pantomime groping through it or having to indicate looking around and under imaginary clothing or other objects. Or looking under a sofa pillow and trying to justify the prop pistol that some other actor has left behind.

Let what you are looking for be a small object. A large object, such as a shoe, may take a half hour to locate at home, but will be difficult to lose in the smaller and barer confines of the studio. Or if your eye goes to your coffee table, which at home was piled with litter but is now bare, you will have a big gap in your "immediacy."

When you have conquered and understood what it was that held you and involved you in each moment of your task, and what allowed you to proceed without anticipation in this exercise, you can apply the same principle to any scene or play. You can also apply it to sending and receiving the words of a play. Someone once said, "A fine actor *forgets* what's coming." He forgets even the next line he has learned until he needs it!

This exercise is easy to understand. It is difficult to execute. Start doing it.

14

THE FOURTH WALL

I REMEMBER a dress rehearsal years ago, when I was a very young actress, during which the entire audience area strongly intruded on my faith and the sense of privacy of my stage room. While playing, I first pretended that no one was out there, and then that no one would ever be, and then that *nothing* was there. Every time I wanted to look up it became more impossible, until I began to hide physically and directed my physical life more and more to the back wall of the set. The director, sitting in the auditorium, stopped the rehearsal with the pronouncement, "Please keep your eyes trained to the balcony-rail level so I can see them." I obliged, played straight out front, and, of course, totally lost a sense of privacy and reality.

If we balk at dishing ourselves out to the audience and making our eyes available to each member of the audience, we ought to balk just as much at hiding. Of course, it is the director's responsibility to ensure that all pertinent action can communicate, and the focus of attention should always be allowed to be controlled by the director, but what can you do for yourself with that big, gaping hole out there which is supposed to be the fourth wall of your set? You can complete it in your imagination as a part of your room or landscape. I know that is easier said than done.

When the play dictates that the audience area must be used for a *primary* purpose it becomes relatively simple to make real. For example, in an outdoor scene, if you are asked to refer to a tree or hill or house or steeple or cloud placed imaginatively out front, and if you have particularized it and anchored it visually to an exit sign or door or a pillar it becomes easy to look at, talk about or point to.

Occasionally, an entire production is devised to break through the proscenium and to make use of the audience area in a primary way. In Elia Kazan's production of *Cat on a Hot Tin Roof,* as the curtain rose, Maggie was standing facing the audience and arranging her hair in an imaginary mirror. This use of the fourth wall was established at once, and then carried out by the other actors with different objects and activities throughout the course of the play.

One of the first things you will discover about an imagined visual object is that you cannot suspend it in midair. Try to. Construct the windowframe visually a few feet away from you, turn your back to it, then face it and try to find it again. It will continually elude you, and your eyes may even cross in your attempt to bring it into focus spacelessly—somewhere. Whatever object you wish to see must be anchored to something which you can see is really there. To start with, you must know the object so well that you can close your eyes and *see* it. Don't try to reconstruct it at the moment of placing it in the auditorium.

Actors challenge me that they can't see anything out front on which to anchor something because it is too dark. Unless a brilliant spotlight is focused directly on you to blind you to the auditorium, this is untrue. We see the outlines of almost everything, from the people to balconies to aisles and exits to the loges at the side and the partitions at the back, etc., etc., while the stage lights are on and the house lights are off.

Actors also challenge me with distance, once they think they have learned to complete a fourth wall by extending the room or landscape into the auditorium, and have placed logical objects out there, and placed them in conjunction with what is really out there: how near or far the imagined objects are *supposed* to be, and how this conflicts with the *actual* distances in the auditorium.

I was ecstatic when I discovered that I could bring anything as near as I wanted or see it a mile away simply by shifting my body accurately. Try it. Look into a mirror to check your appearance when you are only one foot from it, and observe the adjustment of your body to this task. Then do the same thing after you have stepped back six feet. Now check yourself when you look into the mirror from the opposite side of the room. Finally, see if you can re-create all three adjustments by eliminating the mirror and substituting a simple door frame. You will be amazed that you not only believe you see yourself, but that you can bring the mirror close or place it far away without ever moving from the spot simply by finding the focus and re-creating the bodily adjustment to it.

Be sure to place your imaginary objects at the back or sides of the auditorium or in the aisles so that people, still or moving, won't disturb your belief.

You may already have applied this technique successfully to a particular play or production. If not, you will be able to conquer it in a matter of hours. However, if the entire production is *not* conceived to use the fourth wall for a *primary* purpose, beware of doing it all by yourself. If you are the only actor on stage openly relating to imagined clocks, mirrors, pictures, windows, you will seem most peculiar. The audience will probably look behind them to see what you are looking at.

And now we face the problem which most often presents itself—how to exploit fully the fourth wall in a *secondary* way, when we want visual attention to be free to go up and out even though primary inner attention remains connected with the objects on stage, when we don't want to *do* anything to the fourth wall, when we demand of it only that it *be* there for us. We don't want to be walled in or closed off, but liberated by it, free to open up physically without loss of privacy or involvement.

I always set up my *secondary* fourth wall exactly the way I would if I were to use it for a primary purpose. I finish the room, so to speak, by placing imaginary objects that are familiar to me, that have logic and are consistent to the place on that fourth wall of my other three walls, *except* that the objects are secondary in importance. I imaginatively place at least five or six objects across the back and sides of the auditorium, anchoring them to actual objects which exist there. What's in between them seems to take care of itself. My objects must be so particular that I can take them from my mind's eye and place them where I choose. (Don't try to turn an exit sign into a picture, but hang your picture on the exit sign!) I don't need to tell anyone what I'm using. My objects are only there for me, for my privacy, for my freedom from audience intrusion.

Each actor will build his own private fourth wall, since the objects will have no other consequence than on your ability to open up. *They are secondary to everything else on stage.* Distance or physical relationship to them is of no consequence, since you are making no demands on them. For example, while doing something on stage your eye may contact the curtains at the window on your fourth wall. If you should examine them to see if they're hanging straight or need to go to the cleaners, they immediately become primary and an inaccurate divergence from your main purpose onstage. If, while talking or listening, your eye touches on a fourth-wall clock, it's fine, *but* if you contact the clock to see what time it is, the clock immediately becomes primary and defeats your purpose.

In order to experiment with this technique I would like you to take a telephone call as the basic premise of your two-minute exercise. Watch yourself for a few days every time you are at home at your phone to see where your outer, secondary focus goes while your inner attention seems to be given totally to the content of the phone call. When you have settled on the phone call you will use for the exercise, be certain it has all the aspects of the other exercises: time, place, circumstances, objects and objectives. Be sure that your position of standing or sitting at the telephone allows the visual attention to go up and out. (If you are lying on your back on a bed or a sofa, the visual attention normally goes to the ceiling. If you are slouched forward on a chair with your elbows on knees, it would probably go to the floor. If you are at your desk, you may have papers and pencils available, but if the nature of the phone call demands that you make notes or write down what is being said to you be careful that it doesn't take over and prevent your attention from wanting to go up and out.) Whether your circumstances place you already at the phone, or, in the course of them, you decide to make a call or you receive one is unimportant. Just make certain that you are telephoning for the balance of the exercise. You should not improvise the conversation when you present the work, or the fourth wall will not work for you at all. You don't have to write out the dialogue. If you know exactly to whom you are speaking, and what about, and what you want, if you know the content of what is being said to you (not the outer words), and if you rehearse it at least ten times, the words will take on their own inevitability.

After you become aware of the objects which your eyes most often land on while you are telephoning, start to determine how you can set up the same fourth wall in your studio or workshop. When you finally set up the exercise for presentation, take as much time to establish your fourth wall as you would to place your furniture and personal objects in the re-creation of your place. Don't dictate at what points you will look up to make use of the fourth wall. Let the attention go up when it wants to and to what it wants to. Above all, don't *check* if you really see the objects when you look up; that immediately means you are giving them primary importance. When the exercise is successful, the wall will simply *be there* for you in place of the audience. (If a director complains, and suddenly asks what you are looking at out front, you are undoubtedly using fourth-wall objects incorrectly, as primary objects rather than secondarily.)

You may repeat the exercise three or four times with variations of events and kinds of phone calls before it is totally successful. *When* it works, no one will have to tell you so, because you will feel as free as a bird, and relieved of the old agonizing burden of audience intrusion to the point where you will always want to build a fourth wall in every exercise, in every scene on which you work, and for every play in which you will ever appear!

15

ENDOWMENT

THIS probably is the first exercise you will really enjoy working on. It contains the essence of make-believe, and in its simplest form: how to turn cold water into boiling tea or straight brandy or bitter medicine—even hemlock, if you choose; how to remove makeup without cold cream or soap; how to shave without a blade; how to cook or bake without heat; how to eat mashed potatoes and butter without getting fat; how to remove seemingly sodden clothing without having been in the rain, etc.

Reread Chapter 5, "Sense Memory," and then, for the purpose of the endowment exercise, find circumstances under which you would be dealing with tangible objects which would have to be endowed with properties that should not be real on stage. For example, take a cup of water and endow it with the property of steaming hot coffee. Don't just *think* it's hot but recall how, as you bring it toward you, you pull back slightly from the steam, how you carefully blow and puff across the top of the cup to cool the coffee, how you gently test the rim of the cup with your lips before sipping a few drops and gingerly letting the liquid rest on your tongue for a second before allowing it to slide down your throat, how your eyes pull shut as you swallow and your mouth opens and you exhale and then take in air to cool your mouth. Suddenly, that cup of cold water becomes hot coffee and stays that way.

I might not even want to apply real lipstick on stage, because with nervous hands on an opening night it could slip over the edge of my mouth. If there is no room in my stage action for getting cold cream and tissues and fresh powder to repair the damage, I would rather endow a model, plastic lipstick with color and greasiness as I stretch my lips (already made up) and smear it on evenly.

I remember seeing the final dress rehearsal of a play in which a lover was walking out on his mistress. During the course of the action, she had to polish his shoes as one way of preventing his leaving her. The actress was wearing a pearl-gray dress, and the shoe polish was black. As she knelt on the floor, a shoe in one hand, the cloth with polish in the other, the can of black polish on the floor in front of her, she was crying and pleading with him to stay with her. Soon she had globs of polish on her face, hands, and all over her gray costume. It was quite realistic except for one thing. At the end of the scene, the curtain was lowered for only a second and rose again for the next scene which took place a few days later. Her costume and face were still covered with black. In following performances, the inside of the shoe polish can was painted black, without real polish in it, and the actress had found the correct behavior of working with it, the cloth and the shoe, so that not only she but the audience believed she was actually using real polish.

In *The Farewell Supper* by Arthur Schnitzler, I once had to eat an enormous five-course gourmet meal on stage eight times a week. If all the food had been really as specified, I would have been unable to eat it in the time span of my stage life, I would have gained ten pounds a week and probably become sick—certainly on matinee days. What was substituted for the food looked like much more than it was, was neither rich, fattening nor too filling. Endowing the food with sweetness, stickiness, quantity, running juices or butter created a relish for eating, slurping and gulping, and brought me a round of applause as I piled into the final dessert of whipped-cream torte (really mounds of yogurt).

Many scenes call for sewing and threading needles. By now, I look forward to seeing them performed by an inexperienced actor because I know I'm in for some comic relief. The panic which sets in as she takes that small needle and fine silk thread, the variations of attempts to get the thread through the tiny eye, how the thread snarls and knots up, and how she finally ends up pretending and pantomiming sewing because she never could get it threaded are quite predictable. If my needle can't be prethreaded and I *must* do it on stage, I will make certain that the needle I use has the fattest eye in show business; if the thread is to be fine silk, I will use sturdy cotton that won't snarl. If it must seem difficult to thread, I will make it so through endowment, and still be able to control the exact second when the thread will readily go through the eye of the needle. Only if it is a part of the plot that the needle *never* gets threaded, may I use the small needle and the fine thread.

Any object which cannot be handled and controlled readily for the purpose to which you want to put it in your selected action becomes a dangerous object. And there are the actually physically dangerous objects—sharp knives, razors, hot irons, broken bottles, liquor, etc. If it is one of these, I don't expect you to rehearse with it and actually hurt yourself to see what you do about it. You undoubtedly *remember* what it was like when you burned or cut yourself, or otherwise did damage to yourself or were hurt by someone else.

But wherever an object is not physically dangerous, in the sense discussed above, start experimenting—let's say, with polishing your nails (real nail polish on stage could create a major hazard if it spilled or got on your hands). First, really polish your nails, and then take an empty bottle with its little brush and see if you can reconstruct the behavior of carefully and evenly smoothing the polish on your nails until you find such belief that, by reflex, you will blow on your nails to make sure they are dry, and you will handle the next object delicately for fear of marring the polish.

For your exercise, find at least three tangible objects to endow with physical properties which would otherwise control you. You may also endow them psychologically, but the emphasis should rest on the physical. Avoid pantomiming the actions. By that I mean, if you take a stiff drink, don't use an empty glass and then worry about how far to tip it, or what actual swallowing is like. Fill the glass with water and endow the water with whatever properties you need through sense memory and muscular adjustment.

A student occasionally asks if all three endowed objects should belong together. Obviously, they must belong to your complete and logical set of circumstances. If, for instance, your objective is to try to prepare a splendid meal for your lover, and you have a bad cold at the time, endless ideas for objects to endow will immediately occur to you, connected with the food you are preparing, what you will cook it on and what implements you will need for it, as well as all the objects you may need to control your cold, from vaporizers to nose drops to medicines and chest rubs. Just try to give the objects variation so that all three don't involve tasting, or all three don't have to do with hurting yourself, etc. When you have mastered the endowments of the individual objects, give yourself fully to the need for fulfilling your objective with faith in your circumstances in order to avoid simply jumping from one endowed object to the other while checking the accuracy of your execution. When the exercise is ready for presentation, you should have found such trust in your objects that you hardly are aware that they are endowed. They should be wholly there for you.

Any object we deal with, once it has been made particular, will be partially endowed. If I can endow a dull knife with sharpness, I can also endow it further by giving it a history which will dictate even how I pick it up. If the knife was a gift from someone I adore who knows I love to cook—and I am aware that it came from Hammacher Schlemmer's and probably cost about twenty dollars—I will handle it differently than if I physically have to deal with the identical knife and endow it with having been bought at Woolworth's ten years ago, which by accident turned out to be just right and became my favorite old cutting knife.

A rose, which may be wax or plastic on stage, must be not only endowed with the texture, aroma, and thorniness of the real rose in order for me to deal with it with conviction, but will be quite differently dealt with if it is from the favorite plant which I myself grew, or if someone I love gave it to me, or if it is from someone I detest who presented it to me to butter me up. We can and should charge or load each object that we deal with, not only to stimulate our psyche and our senses, but *again* to learn how these elements condition our consequent actions so that when we have to make *selections* for the character's actions in a play, we have discovered all the areas we must draw on to make the selections.

Almost nothing in our character's life *is* what it *is*—but we must make it so! We *endow* the given circumstances, our own character, our relationship to others in the play, the place, each object we deal with, including the clothes we wear. All must be endowed with the physical, psychological or emotional properties which we want in order to send us richly into action from moment to moment.

And so the example of turning an apple into an onion can be a beginning of comprehending that by turning one thing into another, or by supplying missing realities, actions may become sharper than usual, and that reality can be heightened instead of ordinary. It becomes a distilled reality, and that is what I love about it.

Now, you are halfway through the exercises. If you have been actually rehearsing and presenting them for criticism, not just reading about them, you may have discovered their interesting by-products. By now, you are undoubtedly not just rehearsing during the hours you set aside for the exercises, but are "rehearsing" off and on every day. I can't open an oven door without noting how my head pulls back at an angle from the heat. If I'm making a telephone call, a part of me is marking the fourth wall I'm using. Secondary and reflex behavior becomes momentarily conscious. I'm aware of what brought me into a room or out into the street. And the most astounding part of it all is that I don't feel a bit less spontaneous about my behavior. The purpose in establishing habits of self-observation, in discovering the endless variations of behavior which occur from day to day is *not* to reproduce this behavior mechanically *but* . . .

1. To find what inner and outer objects I get involved with under the given circumstances, and why I deal with them.
2. To learn that I do release my psychological and emotional life physically by contacting something else.

3. To discover how my sense of identity changes hourly, depending on needs, surroundings and circumstances, and that these variations in sense of self can be usable for character.

4. To realize what elements are essential in order to bring about two minutes of existence.

I am starting to fill a warehouse for future use in the parts I still hope to play.

16

TALKING TO YOURSELF

THE MONOLOGUE—that old fossil—which has appeared in so many different forms in dramatic literature has always depended on the form that was favored at the time. From century to century, it has adjusted or been cut to fit a current mode of the theater. Whatever its form, it is and has always been a character talking to himself out loud, or to absent characters, or to objects surrounding him at a given time in a given place for a specific reason at a moment of crisis. Whether the emphasis be on the naturalistic or one of selective realism, it is always dependent on whether the relevant content is emotional, psychological, philosophical, poetical, or an amalgam of more than one. Whether the monologue deals with plot or character problems (even if by the author's graces the character is allowed in his eloquence to know more about himself than he actually might in life), or even if the character talks aloud to himself because he is insane, a monologue will always be words representing the character's thoughts or a part of his thoughts. Sometimes it is even the actor's job to persuade himself—and the audience—that these words, or some of them, might actually be inaudible in spite of the fact that they must be heard in the last row of the balcony, or that in life some of the words might be no more than mutterings.

Only when you are talking aloud when *alone* is it a monologue. Anything else is a dialogue! There are entire books of inaccurately titled "monologues" for the actor, consisting of long speeches lifted from plays in which one character talks to another. Someone can *talk back* to you with a look, a snort, a yawn, by turning away, by smiling, by giving you a concentrated look of attention, etc. When a character is called on to talk to the *audience,* it is not a *mono* but a *duo*logue—the audience becomes the actor's partner. (Talking to the audience is discussed on page 207.)

As a mere beginning for the complex problem of talking to *yourself,* I would like you to start to discover and define all the things that make *you* talk aloud to yourself when you are alone, and then present it as an exercise.

Why do we talk to ourselves? *To gain control over circumstances:* To cope with the boredom of a routine or tedious task; to cope with being rattled by time or other pressures, such as frustration and emotional problems, etc. If you are late for an appointment, and are trying to get yourself together as you rush out of the house, and you hear yourself saying, "Where's my key? I've got my gloves. My briefcase is packed. Did I make that call?," etc., as you proceed with the physical tasks of leaving, the verbalization is simply an attempt at organization.

If you are making up a grocery or laundry list, you may verbalize, "Gotta remember the milk. Oh, yes—cranberry juice," etc., and it may help you to remember.

Then there is the kind of fantasy talking aloud which accompanies the boredom of a routine task and manifests itself in comments to and about yourself: "You're stupid. Why did you do it like that?" or "Good girl. You fixed those little eggies nicely." These kinds of comments are often accompanied by oohs and ahs, expletives and grunts. All of these examples are usual and so easy to re-create that I don't suggest you concern yourself with them for the exercise *unless* you think that you never talk to yourself. You *do,* but as it is mostly a subconscious procedure that makes you verbalize, it's possible you are not aware of it. If you think this is true of yourself, by all means start to explore these very basic ways of talking aloud when alone.

If you *know* that you talk to yourself, examine circumstances which go beyond the routine and enter another realm of fantasy. Often while bored by routine tasks, we verbalize fantasies, pretending to be a movie star, royalty, a big boss, a child. We are playing a game. (There's a marvelous example of this at the opening of Elmer Rice's *Dream Girl* when she's getting ready to go to work in the morning.) Haven't you stood at your bathroom mirror completing your toilette and chatted with yourself, switching from Cary Grant to Bette Davis, from self-criticism to self-approval, and kissed yourself in the glass with, "You gorgeous thing, you"?

From there on, the verbalizing gets dramatic! We've had a fight with an agent—or wished we had—and as we come into our apartment, slamming the door, releasing our fury by yanking off our coat, we verbally take it out on the agent. We fantasize what we *should* have said. "Don't you treat me like that, buster, I'm an artist!" We put him down by imitating him. "Really, you did that rather well, but you're not exactly what they want for the part." We reexamine what we *did* say to him. "Oh yes, sir. I understand what you mean. You know these things better than I do."

Or when we are nervous before an audition we practice how we'll impress the director. Or we already assume we've been turned down and start telling him off. "You bastard! Who do you think you are?" We have it out verbally before or after a crisis with colleagues, loved ones, tradesmen, even bus drivers.

What we *don't* do is tell the whole story, or stay in sequence. We *know* what we're talking about, and there is no one there who has to be told what it's about. Consequently, we deal with what disturbs us without the outer logic necessary to make it clear, as we would if another person were listening. All good playwrights know this when they write a monologue. Let the humanness of your behavior reveal the necessary events.

Also, we do not literally, physically act out the words. Our physical life stays connected with the place in which we find ourselves alone; it does not illustrate the life about which we are verbally fantasizing. If I am tidying my desk and having a verbal battle with a friend who bested me last night in an argument in a restaurant, he sits—in my mind's eye—in the restaurant, but *not* in the chair at the other side of my desk. I may flail my papers in the air as I battle with him, but I don't *literally* flail them at the chair across from me.

When Juliet stands on her balcony and talks alone to her Romeo ("Wherefore art thou Romeo?"), he is in her mind's eye at the ball or in the street or in his room, but *not* in that star at which she's staring.

What Juliet is doing on that balcony before, during, in between, and after talking to herself brings me right to the next common mistake which is made by actors, more in actual monologues than in the exercise. The actor very often builds his monologue only around the words and forgets the essential things about his physical presence. I always say, determine what you are doing there *besides* talking to yourself. A verbal life can never have freedom or precision if the body from which the words must spring is inaccurately occupied. I strongly recommend that the scene be found physically *before* you approach the verbal action. Something as general as "I'm in the room waiting for so and so" as an answer to "What were you doing?" has to be made specific by *what* you are *doing* while waiting. Once the physical task is determined, it's easy to contact the inner or outer objects which will propel you into verbalization. Your activities may be temporarily arrested by the verbal life, you may even be diverted from one activity and begin another one, but you do *not* come into a room in order to talk to yourself. You do *not* sit down or rise to talk to yourself. You must know the real reason you do these or other things under your given circumstances in order to allow any verbal fantasy to take shape.

A small dilemma arises for actors, just often enough to deserve clarification. Often, while talking alone, the actor discovers that he "indicates" or verbally dramatizes almost like a bad actor, while dealing with the absent person who has upset him. To a certain degree, a human being exaggerates in order to supply the absent partner; if the person in his mind's eye were really present, he would obviously speak to him quite differently. The actor is nervous about presenting this strange verbal exaggeration for fear it will be misunderstood as plain bad acting. The acting will always remain truthful if it stays within the confines and privacy of the circumstances, but it will definitely be bad acting if it is "indicated" for the audience.

The exercise as it is presented should be of value to you as a start toward many monologues in contemporary, nonpoetic plays. Conquer it before you leave this kind of reality to tackle the deeper and more difficult problems which arise in the heightened realities of poetic drama.

17

OUTDOORS

PART ONE

No MATTER how suggestive or brilliant the set designer may be, the actor, too, must bring the outdoors on stage with him. To achieve it, we must deal with the sensory and physical relationship to space, to nature, as well as their psychological aspects: how we feel about what we see in a sunset, a tree, the ocean or a pond; what is done to us by light, weather, textures of sand, grass, gravel, rock; how we relate to the distance of horizons, what is on them as well as what is between us and them—and what our consequent behavior will be.

To make only a few examples of this exercise, explore circumstances under which you are having a sunbath on the beach, or a picnic in the woods or in a meadow, or stopping for a rest while on a hike in the mountains, or are simply waiting for a friend in the park while the snow is falling or the rain is coming down. Refer to Chapter 5, "Sense Memory," and through remembered sensations find the physical adjustments to what is under you, if you are walking, or sitting in the sand, or on the grass, or on rocks and pebbles. Find your sensations and adjustments to the broiling sun or a soft breeze or a sleety day in February. Know that you must often create *four* fourth walls to surround you, and that the objects you place on them will most likely be of primary importance. Search for your physical and psychological relationship to these objects and to their distance from you (as in the case of the mirror in the fourth-wall exercise on page 108) —objects such as a group of aspen trees, rustling and silvery in autumn light, or a little village with a few white steeples way down below you at the bottom of the hill, or crashing surf on the reef straight ahead of you.

When you have completed an exercise of this kind successfully you will have become aware of your relationship to nature and to space so that you will deal with them actively. You might even become aware, as you look out of your window down into the street, that your upper body stretches forward and your shoulders pull back as your neck cranes in an arch, if you really want to see way down and out. You won't need to schedule rehearsal hours for practicing—you'll just do it.

PART TWO

In all of the prior exercises we have been exploring the use of outer objects as well as inner objects to achieve an objective under clearly defined circumstances: the specific objects of our daily existence, even seemingly unimportant ones like ashtrays, pillows, crockery, bottles, pots, pans, cutlery, books, papers, magazines, etc. We have discovered how we dealt with them for a primary purpose, or how they rounded out our existence in a secondary, even involuntary way. We should have found a new sense of reality and been freed of self-consciousness or tension coming from the awareness of being observed—all that makes us *be* a human being, not an "actor." *But* what happens when the playwright says, "A hill near Dublin," or "A country road—A tree—Evening," or "A room in the palace. An archway, a pillar, a bench," or "A street in Verona"? No tangible objects are mentioned. Suddenly we are actors on stage again instead of characters (people) in life. Even highly skilled actors become tense and look for stances and postures in an effort to protect themselves against a feeling of unreality or spacelessness.

In order to tackle this problem at its roots, see what you actually *do* when you are removed from all the goodies of the living room, kitchen and bath, when there are no emotional or physical crises to deal with, when you don't even have a picnic or rain or a crossword puzzle or sun lotion or a book to explore or deal with. Suppose you are waiting for a vehicle or a person outdoors or on a deserted subway platform. There are no major obstacles. You aren't late. It's a routine appointment you are bound for. The weather is normal. You have nothing with you except perhaps your purse or a briefcase. Nothing tangible is near you except possibly a bench. In other words, you have stripped away all of the things which ordinarily suggest countless things to do while waiting. (If you *sit* on the bench during the balance of the waiting, you will bypass the real problem of the exercise.)

Before selecting your particular place and circumstances for the exercise, watch what you do every time you stand for a few minutes waiting outside when most alone, such as at a bus stop at an hour when other people aren't waiting with you, or on a subway platform at a nonrush hour, or in an isolated section of a park while waiting for someone. (Avoid the problems of technically working for your eyes following moving traffic or indicating reactions to imaginary people.) Your primary action will have to do with the expected arrival of the vehicle or person. You'll immediately discover that you don't stand rigid or immovable while waiting. In between the primary action of checking the possible approach of the vehicle or person and contacting the inner objects which have to do with your destination or meeting—where you're going, who you're going to meet, and what you'll do when you get there—you will be secondarily occupied with what is on you (clothing) and around you, as well as with the secondary inner objects of past, present, and future.

Example: 9:30 P.M. at the 6th Avenue and 23rd Street subway stop. You are on your way home from a scene rehearsal with a partner. A young couple are waiting way down at the other end of the platform. It is late fall, and you are wearing slacks and a sweater, a light sports coat and carrying a shoulder bag. A friend of yours has a part in an episode of a TV series, and it is on in half an hour. You go to the edge of the platform and lean forward to look down the tunnel to see if the train is coming. You are poised to listen for the sound of the train. No luck. You walk back a few steps and adjust your shoulder bag. You remember last week's segment of the television series and the announcement of your friend's appearance. You examine your sneakers and consider getting new ones. Your attention is drawn to a crack in the cement, and you try to walk along it without teetering. You check for the train again, etc., etc. There is a continuous flow of attention and adjustments between inner and outer objects, between primary and secondary objects coming from your objective, and your past, present, and future circumstances. (How much you do while you *think* you do nothing! How many things Vladimir and Estragon do while *waiting*—for Godot!)

It must be obvious to you that the more precise and total your surroundings and circumstances are, the easier it will be for you to achieve a free-flowing attention from one object to another. You cannot give them a regimented order or you will immediately deal with them artificially and with tension. You must construct your four walls so well that your outer focus is free to go where it wants to, and you must examine *yourself* as an object and what's on you with detail. Your initial entrance or physical being—standing or sitting—what you do, is also conditioned by what you wear (what's comfortable or uncomfortable, what's old or new, what's tacky or elegant, etc.).

It should be a new experience for you to *be* for two or three minutes without any feeling of being boring, or tense, or self-conscious while you are being observed.

The difficulty in applying the exercise to a character on stage, which sometimes occurs even after the exercise has been thoroughly understood, arises because the actor has failed to make his "costume" his clothes; the garden of his "palace" as real and precise as his park; the objects coming from past, present and future as real and familiar to him as those which sprang from his own life and experience. But for the time being, learn to see what *you* do when you just "stand and wait."

18

CONDITIONING FORCES

Sense memory has been explored and given emphasis for different purposes in both the endowment and outdoor exercise. A more complex problem arises when we have to deal with more than one sensation at the same time, such as when we have a headache *and* a backache. A hangover can include a queasy stomach, a bad taste in the mouth, and a heavy head. For other conditions which influence our behavior (such as darkness or glare, quiet, hurry, etc.) and which might be part of the given circumstances employ the same technique as for sense memory. We might well find ourselves in circumstances where three or four, even five of them exist simultaneously.

In Sean O'Casey's *The Bedtime Story*, the hero wants desperately to get a whore out of his house before his roommate returns. He is Catholic, feels he has sinned, and the idea of discovery is more than he can bear. The whore has promised to get up and out if he finds her lipstick which she left somewhere in the living room. In his search, he knocks over a vase and floods the floor, his feet, and his shoes which are under the table. For fear of discovery he won't turn on the light, and he is terrified that the landlady downstairs may hear him. The room is bitter cold, and he can't find a shilling to put into the meter of his heating unit. In short, the actor is faced with hurry, cold, quiet, darkness and wet. He has to juggle five conditions at once.

I call these "conditioning forces" because the scene is rarely *about* the hurry, the darkness, the cold, etc., but the action is conditioned by them.

No one wants to wait until he is hired for a part and has to face rehearsals for a difficult character to learn how to deal with many conditioning forces. When you first consider possibilities for this exercise it may seem like being asked to pat the top of your head while you rub your stomach, but after you learn how to stagger them, it will be relatively simple to accomplish.

I've discussed how to work on a variety of physical sensations individually, and how to work for moving about in the dark, but I've saved how to be in a hurry until now. The change in behavior when only a few minutes' difference are at stake is one of my favorite classroom demonstrations. I *adore* performing it.

1. I am at home, finishing my morning's crossword puzzle and coffee before going to teach my 11 o'clock class. I live about nine blocks from the Studio. I check the time and discover that it is 10:50. Obviously I am in a hurry. I put down my pencil and the puzzle. I take up my purse and classbook. I grab my coat and run out the front door hoping there will be a taxi right outside, because then I will certainly be on time. My rush has a kind of neat and precise organization. I'm still in control of it. Not a move has been wasted.

2. Everything is as before up to the point where I look at my watch. This time it is 10:55. I grab for my purse, puzzle still in hand. I bump the catch so that the purse opens and some of the contents fall on the floor. Totally disorganized, I

run for my coat and then back to the purse. I try to retrieve some of the stuff from the floor, leave half of it there. I take the puzzle with me, forgetting my classbook. I catch the sleeve of my coat on the door, leaving a button behind as I rush out. I have a very small chance of getting to the Studio on time, but I am already speculating on excuses in case I am late.

3. Identical circumstances except that when I check my watch it is 11 A.M. I don't believe it. I look at the time again—*hard!* Rage sets in. My whole soul seems to be in a hurry, but I *slowly* put aside my pencil and the puzzle. I rise with enormous deliberation. I pick up my purse firmly by the handle, and take my classbook under my arm. I reach for my coat and stop to put it on. I give the last button a yank and stomp out the door, banging it hard behind me.

So, if I really want to find the behavior which is influenced by time, I must be precise about my destination as well as my expectancy as to the amount of time it will take to get there.

The necessity to be quiet, which is a condition of so many scenes, almost takes care of itself *if* you not only know precisely why you must be quiet, but have an orientation to the distance away from the person or persons whom you don't wish to disturb, plus an expectancy of what you *think* they could hear or what might disturb them at that distance. Put someone in another room in your house, and with your knowledge of the distance and the degree of sound which you *think* can penetrate to that other room, see how you can accomplish a task so they won't hear you. Try it once when you assume that they're busy with their own task in the other room, and then when you assume they're asleep. How "quietly" you execute your own task will vary accordingly. In other words, the condition must be established with the necessary components in order to allow you to believe in it.

Correctly achieved, this sensation is so suggestive that an actor often continues to tiptoe after his exercise is completed. It is in his bones, so to speak, and has set up reflexes which he deals with almost involuntarily. That's ideal and can actually be achieved with all the conditions!

No condition or sensation is static or remains with you to the same degree of intensity. It varies, depending on the nature of the action. It may even be momentarily forgotten until another action reminds you of it again.

If you complicate the *task* of this exercise you will have difficulty not only in executing the conditions but even in finding enough of them which might exist during the given action. As an example, set yourself the objective of getting ready to go out to meet someone at the art movie house in the neighborhood. You still have to finish dressing, fix your face and hair, and get together some money from various pockets, drawers and piggy banks. First, work through the actions and deal with all the objects without any extra conditioning forces until the task has logic, and you are thoroughly familiar with each object you have to handle for a purpose.

Now consider a number of conditions—heat or cold, a hangover, quiet, hurry, a toothache, a blister on your heel, a head cold. Start with a condition which is suggestible to you. Possibly you imagine that the apartment is overheated and stuffy. Your blouse is sticking to your shoulder blades. You loosen it and puff a little. Now head for your objective to see in which way the heat influences each doing of getting your shoes on, fastening your belt, adjusting your collar. How does it influence trying to fix your face if your face is sticky or perspiring? Is your hair damp at the nape of your neck so that the curls droop as you try to comb them, etc.? When the heat is in your bones so that you can't forget it, and yet don't have to give it conscious attention any longer, *add* another condition. A headache. How does the throbbing intensify when you lean down for your shoes? What do you do to ease it? What happens to your head when you pull the comb through the damp locks or across the top of your head, etc.? When the headache is there for you, embedded in the actions with specific adjustments, *add* hurry. You expect that your friend is already in the lobby of the movie house and that the feature will start in a few minutes. Obviously, the nature of the heat and the headache will be influenced by the hurry.

When the adjustments to the conditions have been made specifically in conjunction with the task, your reflex behavior should take care of the rest. If this works for you successfully, be brave and add a fourth and then perhaps even a fifth condition. If it is difficult, as it probably will be in the beginning, repeat the exercise after criticism, over and over again, trying different tasks and conditions until it becomes a correct and ingrained work habit.

The order in which you stagger and rehearse the conditions does have relevance, I think. Start with the one you think has least importance so it can stay there in your bones as a reflex, and end up with the one to which you have to give the most conscious attention. (It is hard to "shelve" nausea in the subconscious.) In this way you will avoid having to "think" of too many things at once.

When the exercise has succeeded, you may feel that you've been as busy as a great cook who has prepared a gourmet meal. But then you will have the right to announce to your peers or to your teacher, "Bon appetit, this is Julia Child!"

19

HISTORY

WE BRING a concept with us from childhood which seems to be difficult to overcome even as we mature. It continues to exist despite a good education. For some strange reason, we believe that anyone who lived before we were born was in some peculiar way a different kind of human being from any we have come in contact with in our own lifetime. This concept must be changed; we must realize in our bones that almost everything in time and history has changed *except* the human being. He has changed outwardly. His outer habits and customs, appetites, manners and points of view have changed through the sociological forces which have influenced him. But we have all been born in similar ways, have had to sustain ourselves with food and drink, sleep and exercise, have had loves and hates, greeds and envies, etc., and have died in similar ways. And when we choose, or are called on, to play a character living in a time that precedes our own birthday, we must still find the human being and not a cardboard cliché. The almost automatic cliché image connected with a costumed figure should be discarded.

On pages 29 and 30 in the chapter on "Identity," I went

into this problem, briefly though vehemently. I don't believe we should be willing to accept convenient or stale traditions. Remember all the Hamlets, Gertrudes, Tartuffes or Misanthropes, the Candidas or Important Ernests, the Heddas and Vanyas you have seen who never ate or slept or even breathed like human beings—whether they were presented in summer stock or college or community theaters, whether they were seen off or on Broadway. They are usually as lifeless as the figures in a wax museum. I believe deeply that we should rebel against these traditions and bring these characters to an audience alive!

If you read a play by Oscar Wilde and immediately see yourself in "result" terms assuming the manner of the play, does this image of false elegance come from what you've already seen on stage, or can you give it roots by finding what was important to the fashion of the times (something as trivial as pouring tea from a silver, ebony-handled teapot without leaving a fingermark on it into a dainty bone-china cup from just the right height so that there will be only a few bubbles in the tea, and so that as you pour, the lace ruffle at your wrist will fall properly and that your tight, silk sleeve will not be too strained at the elbow) in order to prove that you belong to the elite of London society? Will you, as a man, put on the tights of Hamlet to find an acceptable *pose*, or will you put them on as the clothing which belongs to you and in which you live and walk and sit and run? Will you make a hoopskirt yours by finding its sensory reality and physical assets and problems, by giving it a history of when you bought it, whether it's new or old, whether it's the finest or the poorest, etc.?

In this, as well as in the next (and last) exercise, I ask you for the first time to use a specific character from a given play, rather than solely using yourself and your own life experience. (In studying acting, you will not be doing only these exercises, but in between you will surely be working on scenes from plays. Therefore, I am taking it for granted that you will have some idea of the examination of a character so that the selection you make for these last two exercises will not be willful, but will be made from true considerations for, and identifications with the specific character.) Select a character that interests you from a play you consider to be historical in time. I don't necessarily mean an actual historic figure like Napoleon or Henry VIII or Elizabeth I, but a character from any play predating your sense of "now." Determine the time and place your character lives in and begin your research.

Keep as much of your research as possible on a subjective level, and continuously look for an identification with it. Discover the customs and habits and manners of the time and place, the social and political influences on the people, the architecture and households, the furnishings and clothing of the time. The channels to travel which will most stimulate the imagination are individual. As I have said before, biographies of personalities of a given time stimulate me most. Paintings, literature, poetry and music of the time can be eye-openers, while I find dates of battles and treaties to be of little value. The sources you use should allow you to begin to believe that you are existing at that time in that place, not only by identifying with the larger events of the time, but with all aspects of living from day to day. Go to the library and to museums, and begin to look—look with your present-day eyes for what truly matters. Select!

Having done as much research as you can, take your character out of crisis in the play and give him roots by placing him in a daily event. Give him a simple task. Don't paraphrase or make melodrama or rewrite the dramatic events of the play. You want to make certain your character eats, sleeps, washes, dresses, walks, perhaps runs!

Example: Nina (*The Sea Gull*), in her bedroom, preparing herself for an outing at the lake; the life of a landowner's daughter outside Moscow in the late 1800's. You must look for, and identify with, and make use of not only your (Nina's) clothing and underclothing, the details of your room (washbowls with pitcher and soap and heavy linen towels, the kind of bed and bedding, curtains, scrubbed flooring, icons, prayer habits) but also with what you read, what's forbidden or allowed. How do you write? By candlelight, kerosene, gaslight? If you write a note to Konstantin, on what kind of paper, with what kind of pen and ink, etc.? Then explore your specific task of getting ready for an outing.

You may well ask if this isn't an awful lot of work and research (weeks and possibly months of it) for a two-minute exercise. But the work goes way beyond the exercise itself. If you want to get literal, remember how many plays in dramatic literature concern themselves with Russia at the end of the nineteenth century! If you explore the life of one character at the turn of the sixteenth century in London, you may uncover the historic realities of a hundred plays. But more important, you will be learning that by eliminating historic distance and strangeness for one period, you will be able to do it for any other. You will learn that you can make yourself believe that you exist at another time in another place in a very rudimentary way.

Take Brutus readying himself for a council meeting. Even if you achieve only believing that you often *really* wear a toga, you will have learned a great deal. Explore Desdemona getting ready for, or coming back from, a Venetian ball, before she met Othello. Or Roderigo preparing for bed. Or Horatio studying for an exam at Wittenberg. Et cetera.

Let me make clear that I do not expect you to rent or sew an accurately detailed costume, or to rent furniture or other physical properties of the historical time (or to steal them from a museum!). Part of your exploration will involve the endowments of readily constructed or available clothing and objects with the shapes and textures of the time until they not only seem accurate to you but truly become yours. How they outwardly look to an observer is irrelevant for this purpose. (That is ultimately the designer's and the director's job.) But they should allow you to believe and consequently behave accurately for the character in the given time and place.

This journey back into time will be—only momentarily—like visiting an unfamiliar country—*now*.

20

CHARACTER ACTION

RETURN to my original premise that you must learn to expand your image of self (enlarge your sense of identity) in order to use yourself to be somebody else, to avoid illustration of a preconceived outer image of the character. Take stock of what you have done in the exploration and presentation of all the object exercises leading up to this one. You ought to be ready to test the selection of actions belonging to a character in a specific play; to test how you can make a lie into truth, fiction into reality, by using your own being.

There is an old adage claiming, "Tell me what you *do*, and I'll tell you who you *are*." Or the story of the farmer who has plowed his fields, and then washes up and cleans his fingernails before eating his stew. He is quite a different character from the farmer who simply plows his fields and then eats. The selection of actions as well as their sequence reveals the specific human being. To begin to put this theory into practice in its simplest form is the premise of the last exercise. Once again you can work on it and prepare it for presentation without a partner. How many characters you explore, and how often you present the exercise for criticism is up to you, but it can go on ad infinitum.

Choose two characters you might play who live in the same country at approximately the same time (now, or in history). They might even be two characters from the same play. Remove them from the events of the play and put them in a place in which they might both find themselves, giving them a common, simple objective with similar circumstances. Then select objects with which they might each occupy themselves under these circumstances, and attempt to construct the behavior logical to each character by changing your endowments of the objects they deal with which would serve each character.

Consider *yourself* as an object and clothe yourself with basic elements which can be endowed differently to serve the two different characters. For example, Blanche and then Stella (*A Streetcar Named Desire*) in the family doctor's outer office waiting for an annual routine check-up on a humid August afternoon in Laurel, Mississippi. Both have come from a bridge luncheon. Both could wear a linen summer suit, a chiffon kerchief at the neck, pumps over silk stockings, and be carrying a small leather purse. Both pick up *Redbook* magazine and look at it, arrange the contents of their purses, correct their makeup, drink from the water cooler, smoke a cigarette. You must find the sensory and emotional relationship to each object which might serve you for each character. And now put yourself in motion. Trust only the real action; if you are really *doing*, you are in action.

Blanche. You had your hair and nails done before the luncheon. Your nail enamel is a new color. Your hair is a little damp at the nape of your neck, and the curl is starting to fall. The perky scarf around your neck is drooping a bit. The seam at the back of your silk stockings is in perfect order, and the pumps are as white as snow. Your makeup is a bit caked and oily, but the girls at the party complimented you on your slimness and your suit. You check the old leather couch for dust before sitting down. The copy of *Redbook* is a little sticky with the fingermarks of others, and you deal with the pages gingerly, and hold the magazine away from your lap as you look at the photos of a few celebrities. You open your purse to get a hanky to wipe your fingers. A little loose tobacco at the bottom of your purse annoys you, and you pick it out. You open your compact and try to smooth out the little wrinkles at the corners of your mouth and eyes, first with Kleenex and then with your powder puff. You dab off the smudged lipstick and smooth on the fresh. You try to liven up the kerchief at your neck so you'll be at your best for the charming doctor. You take a drink from the cooler, and after watching the sharp little bubbles in the icy water you take small sips from the paper cup. You sit down again and put a cigarette into an ivory holder before lighting it and waiting patiently for the doctor.

Stella. Almost everything is the same. The bridge party was friendly but boring. You ate a bit too much. Your feet are hot, so you slide out of your pumps and rest your feet on the trodden heels. You look for the continuation of last month's love story in *Redbook* and after finding it you tear out the pages, fold them, and put them in your purse. You take out your compact and check your face. You wipe some perspiration from your forehead with a tissue, and rub off your caked lipstick, leaving your lips smooth and shiny without putting on any fresh color. You get a big gulp of water from the cooler. You stand in front of the noisy old fan and loosen your jacket to let some air blow in. You pull off your tacky scarf, light a cigarette, and then go to the doctor's door and knock to remind him that you are waiting.

You might choose Felix and Oscar (*The Odd Couple*) getting ready for a date, or checking into a hotel. They have such human elements of fastidiousness and untidiness that I find it easy to identify with both of them—even though I am not a man—and have experienced tendencies toward both elements to excess, depending on the surrounding circumstances and events.

You will present both the characters you have chosen, one after the other, in the same place and circumstances, using the same objects with a similar objective. The trap is to "make sure they're very different from each other," which might lead to watching the action instead of giving yourself to the *needs* with your differently endowed objects. Always allow the behavior to ensue through *you*. Successfully executed, you will be *you*—both times—even though an observer might hardly recognize you in either of the characters.

Each of the ten object exercises should be rehearsed and presented often enough to convince you that you have understood and solved the individual technical problem it concerns itself with. If you have completed them all, you can continue with endless combinations: (1) a phone call to your parents or friends giving a party, in which you talk to two or more persons successively, to discover how you change according to the relationship you have to the person on the other end of the phone; (2) finding a lost object with staggered conditions; (3) talking to yourself under circumstances where endowed objects are necessary; (4) a historic character outdoors; (5) continuous use of a secondary or primary fourth wall, etc.

Continue disciplined work habits and stretch yourself by setting higher and higher goals for yourself.

And now—the play!

PART THREE

THE PLAY AND THE ROLE

INTRODUCTION

For many years, I used the word organic *when speaking about acting: to work organically, to perform organically, to bring about an organic human being. To me it meant creating something alive and from within, as opposed to leaping at illustrations of something preconceived. Webster defines the word as "pertaining to or derived from living organisms; exhibiting characteristics belonging to human organisms." Since the advent of an awareness of ecology, the word has taken on added emphasis as applied to farming and gardening. In this sense, it means to make use of nature's own gifts and habits by learning them, understanding them, and putting them to use without adding anything synthetic, chemical or artificial. I love the idea that whether I make a rose or a role grow big and healthy I must do it organically.*

In the next seven chapters, I am proposing the various stages of work on a role, all of the areas we must explore before arriving at the final selection of actions for the specific character. I want to emphasize that the working steps must be flexible. Even though you want a degree of order and logic in developing your character, don't box yourself in or rely on "rules." Don't look for labels or assume that each chapter can be filed away or considered "done!" until you can fuse them all into a living role. Creativity—based on freedom, and freedom based on responsibility, as in life—does not follow a rigid formula.

Chapters 21 through 27 embrace, I hope, all the areas you should examine to unearth the character. They will overlap. In the working process, one may precede another. But whatever you begin with, wherever you put the emphasis, the work must lead you to the action, to the spontaneous doing, giving body and substance to the playwright's and the director's dream, and convincing the audience that this dream is lucid and real.

The masterful technique of a genius consciously employs these areas of work only when the intuition fails and he doesn't know what to do next. Great actors have accumulated the substance of these chapters, almost subconsciously, but we must learn these techniques and begin our work with a kind of blueprint based on them. When we use the blueprint well, the tracings will not show in the final architecture. Our structure must stand free and be ready to be lived in.

21

FIRST CONTACT WITH THE PLAY

WHEN an actor first reads the play on which he is going to work, he is an audience. He visualizes the play and hears it like an audience. Whatever identification he may have with the play is similar to the identification an audience might have, and should not be confused with the organic identification he must find with the character he is going to play. He laughs at or with the play, he cries at or with the play, and, more than anything else, he cries and laughs at or with the character he is going to play. This is a normal reaction. At this point, he *is* the audience. He is still on the other side of the footlights; he is not yet on stage. This is why the images he conceives, and the tones and sounds he hears in his imagination on his first contact with the play must soon be discarded and not confused with the real work on the play and the part. The actor still has to go backstage and then evolve on stage.

Whenever I retained my first images or used them as guidance for my character I was in big trouble. However, when I worked subjectively through the play from its roots— to discover who "I" am, what "I" want, what "I" do—I ended up with something quite different, with deeper human meaning and no ready-made clichés. Jumping for the illustration of the first image is almost an automatic trap for the inexperienced actor. It may even manifest itself in something as obvious as crying at the moment when he feels sorry for the character, though the character himself wouldn't shed a tear. The actor is providing the tears that eventually should be in the eyes of the audience. It doesn't necessarily mean that the character is moved. The character is in action, struggling.

With this in mind, read the play once. And then again and again. This may seem self-evident and naïve, but I can point to many examples where a sloppy actor "just loved" a scene he was observing in class and wanted to know "What's it from?" He had to be told it was from the same play from which he'd done a different scene only the week before!

Ask yourself what the playwright wants to communicate. Define it in an active sentence. Whether or not your definition is correct will finally be the director's decision or an agreement between the two of you. However, you should grasp this approach so that when the director shapes a production thematically in order to further the playwright's intention, you will be able to respond correctly and understand that he is asking you to help him execute this theme.

A play like *A Streetcar Named Desire* might be interpreted as a plea for the sensitive: the problem of a hypersensitive romantic victim of a brutal society. It may ask the audience for compassion for its victim. In this interpretation, Blanche would be the protagonist of the play; Stanley the antagonist; Stella fluctuating and caught between; Mitch, beginning by joining with the protagonist, but ending up against her; the poker players siding with the antagonist; the newsboy with the protagonist; and the neighbors caught between. You would immediately have "sides" for and against, consequently the rudiments of necessary basic relationships of the characters—not only to the play but to each other. In fact, the play *was* produced with this theme.

The play has *also* been produced as a plea for a down-to-earth, rational life by a director who envisioned a healthy, animal society represented by Stella and Stanley and their friends. Into this society a highly destructive and neurotic Blanche enters from a sick world of the past to destroy this functioning society, undermining the very fiber of Stella's and Stanley's lives. Consequently, the relationships of the characters to the play and to each other become diametrically opposed.

It should become obvious that in order for the individual actor to make a meaningful contribution to the play—to bring about a character to serve this play—he must learn to make considerations about the play itself before he begins to "interpret" or make a layout for his own role willfully, at random, or simply to serve his own ego.

A side effect and a danger of studio work (where the actor is learning to study parts with a teacher whose function must be to teach him how to work on parts, to make him real in the execution of parts, but *not to direct* him in his parts) is that the actor may get into the habit of "interpreting" alone, so that when he *does* work with a director he feels intruded upon. He may then feel that the director is putting his finger into his "creation," actually interfering with the actor's creative process. This is a terrible misunderstanding. A correctly trained actor should not only need and want a director to help him, to lead him into and through the play up to the final editing and selection of action, but should have at his fingertips a technique so flexible that he can justify almost any direction he is given, and execute it in terms of his personal realities. He should be able to do the internal work which will bring about the externals demanded by the director. The acquisition of a good technique should make it possible to execute anything. The responsibility lies in the execution.

My first year as a teacher consisted of my mistakenly "helping" the actor by giving him a directorial score rather than dealing with his technical problems as an actor. After his scene had been interpreted and directed for him, the actor not only felt better, but looked better to his colleagues —but only for that scene! At the end of the semester he had the identical difficulties with which he'd begun. His execution of a scene was dependent on *my* technique instead of on the development of his own.

In the continued examination of the play there is a mixture of objective and subjective research. The objective ought to consist of about ten percent and the subjective the other ninety percent. Whatever intellectual work takes place *at any stage of the game* should serve to stimulate the creative imagination but *not* make for an essay or master's thesis on the play or the character.

After examining possible themes for the play and deciding on your answer to "What does the play want?" (which should give you a sense of where you are going), examine the events of the play in terms of time and place and human needs and conflicts. If you are sensitive, you will also get an impression of the texture of the play, and this should free your intuitions about it and your role. The play might be earthy, robust, like sienna, like a field of yellow hay, like Mahler, etc. Or it might be like clear water, sparkly, with sharp, icy particles, or a translucent blue, like Mozart, etc. These descriptions are meaningful to me. They help me to select personal actions. If you find similar things which stimulate you, make use of them. But don't discuss them. Don't get mystical or general about them. Everything you explore should eventually lead you to real walking, talking, seeing, hearing, smelling, tasting, touching—and feeling!

I like to make notes on the play. If anyone else read them they wouldn't have the vaguest idea what the notes meant. My notes are highly personal and have to do with my own life experiences, things which might be useful as anchors or substitutions for identification with my character and relationships. My notes also have to do with my state of being at various times in my life which might relate to the events of the play. I make my notes at random as things occur to me. Some of them I extend and others I forget. I continuously make new notes.

Having explored this area for better or worse, I will now move on to the next real question: Who am I in this play?

The specialized vocabulary we use to describe technical problems in acting has endless interpretations—sometimes opposing ones—so many that I'd like to resort to one of my favorite handbooks on acting: the dictionary! I have selected the definitions given by Mr. Webster which best help me to describe what I *mean* by them. For example, under the noun "Play" only the ninth definition states, "A dramatic composition or performance." I like the first and second even better. 1. "The action, motion, especially when free, rapid or light." 2. "Freedom or scope for motion or action." I will begin the following chapters with Webster's definitions, and star (*) my preferences.

22

THE CHARACTER

char′ac·ter 1. a distinctive mark, trait, quality or attribute. *5. the aggregate of distinctive qualities belonging to an individual impressed by nature, education or habit. *6. essential quality, nature; kind. *7. an individual's pattern of behavior or personality, moral constitution. 9. reputation. 15. person in a play, story, novel, etc.

Oh . . . to *be* Hamlet! Ahhh . . . to *be* Juliet! To be St. Joan, or Eliza Doolittle, or 'Enry 'Iggins for the few hours allotted by the playwright! If you really want to *be,* you'd better know who you are when the play begins, and how you got to be that way!

The cliché image from the first reading of the play still dangles in front of me. I still see "her" running into her lover's arms, or retreating shyly into a corner of the room. I can hear "her" melodious voice with the slight regional accent, and I am yearning to try those poetic moments from the second act out loud, to get on my feet in my own living room and imitate my vision of "her." It's a dangerous lure.

When I confront the character I'm going to play, I must ask myself, "Who am *I?*"

I must begin organically by finding a change of address and a new autobiography. If I ask myself, "Who is *she?*" and "Where was *she* born?" I might end up with a brilliant treatise on someone possibly more removed from me than when I began. Rather than closing the gap between myself and the character, I may have created an abyss. The difference between the "she" and the "I" is crucial. Dublin 1865, for "her" is a convenient and easily dismissed fact. If, however, my first question is where and when was "I" born, and the answer in the play is Dublin, 1865, the answer becomes loaded with new questions for which I must find answers and substitutions, using my imagination to make them *serviceable* facts.

My aim is to give myself new roots, to make all of the elements of "my" life up to the play's beginning as concrete as I can, until I know as much as possible about the new "me" and more than "she" knows about herself. I must even investigate "my" subconscious needs and the things I don't want to face about "myself." I must glean (from intensive study of the play) facts about parents, upbringing and education, health, friends, skills and interests. I should not only begin to weigh what "I" say and do (and why), but also what others say about "me," and how they respond to me, what these things reveal about "my" main drives as a human being, what "I" want as well as what "I" don't want. Later, all of this must feed and fill what I contact inwardly, as well as what I actually see and hear, and whatever may move in on me. This should make me understand what I do, and why I must do it. And it should give me the faith that "I" *am!*

A scoffing actor asked, "Why in the world do you have to know who your grandmother is?" I answered, "It can't hurt; it might help!" As someone once said (God help me if I remember who it was. I hope it was me!), "All tedious research is worth one inspired moment."

In order to construct a new life up to the time when the play begins, use imaginative identification with all the facts you can sift out of the play by substitution or by using the magic "If I . . ."

When I worked on the part of Georgie Elgin in Clifford Odets' *The Country Girl,* I devoured the play for any light it could shed on "my" background. I—Georgie—was born in Hartford, Connecticut, about thirty years ago into a middle-class society. My parents, with airs, gave me an education in private schools. The play tells me that my mother was socially ambitious, gardened for a hobby, was unaffectionate, and that I consciously rejected all the things she thought important. My father was a prominent performer, a magician. He seemed illusive to me—away from home on tours much of the time. I admired him and his need for freedom from a narrow, conventional life. At an early age, I married a known actor who was considerably older than I. The marriage seemed to be good for a short time. Then my husband's enjoyment of alcohol became a disease. We had a child who died young. The death gave him another excuse for drinking and brought him and me near skid row. His dependence on me grew, and so I stuck by him. I have no friends, have isolated myself more and more from others. I find an outlet in books. These are some of the things I can discover about my past life from the play itself.

Before these facts can be really useful to me I have to round them out with an imaginative question-and-answer game. Wherever I can draw on my own experience to meet those of Georgie I will do so. If my own life strongly differs in any area, I'll borrow from observation or make substitutions. I want this past to have such a reality that even my reflexes on stage will be those of "me"—Georgie Elgin.

Georgie's mother has no connection with my own, so I try the next best thing and use the mother of an early schoolmate who fills the bill. She was a woman with silvery hair set in artificial waves, with orange-lacquered nails and a passion for bridge. I remember identifying with my friend (her daughter) as she was dismissed, pushed aside, and made into a convenient "sweet thing." I enlarge my imagined life with her into daily events of coming home from school, having dinner, preparing for bedtime, etc.

I can make a more direct transference of my father to Georgie's father. I use a direct image of my own father, his enormous work concentration and freedom and aloneness in that work, and I change his work from writing to magic tricks. I must now mate him with my new mother. I use how I put him on a pedestal, how I treasured our few moments alone when he shared his work with me, how we escaped together from that mother. By combining real and imagined people and incidents, I am laying a groundwork for my new character.

Madison, Wisconsin, where I grew up can be transferred to Hartford, Connecticut—even the school, the church, the country club, and aspects of my own home. I also visited Hartford, so my faith in the transference is strong. From her vocabulary, her choice of expressions, as well as the playwright's statement, I know that Georgie is a bookworm. I recall my own need to barricade myself with Shaw and Chekhov to get away from my prom and sorority acquaintances, and now use Georgie's Whitman, the Brontes, and Jane Austen instead. I continue to build my early life, and consider its consequence on my present one.

Did the seeming illusiveness of "my" father, and my love for him make me fall in love with an older man, a man who was also a performer? Did "my" mother's ambition for a certain kind of social status make me rebel and see only its falseness? I become aware that "my" refuge in books still sustains me in my present sordid life.

I am bound to meet up with problem areas in which these kinds of substitutions are not easily available. One such problem area is the complexity of my relationship to my husband, Frank. *Exactly* what attracted me about him? What was the nature of our courtship? Was I immediately aware of his great talent, not just seduced by his fame? Did it make me feel stronger to hold him up after drinking bouts? Did I, perhaps, have a baby to give him a greater sense of responsibility? How often have I tried to break away from him, and what did he have to do each time to seduce me into staying? Was the relationship sexually powerful at first? When did I become aware that he lied and cheated to win me around, and that his lying worked on me like one of my father's magic tricks? When did his drinking and inability to hold a job become the intolerable burden on me that exists as the play opens? What made me accept and enjoy the first drinks with him? Were they a part of my intoxication with him as a man and an artist? Did they enhance my sexual intoxication with him? When, what and where was the turning point which turned the enjoyment into an aversion? What incidents helped me to shape a main objective and character drive of putting up a death battle to hold onto my personal integrity and sense of dignity?

The *answers* I must give to these kinds of questions are consequential only to me. Each actress who tackles the part of Georgie will find different answers and make her own substitutions.

Other problem areas will arise. What do I use for the loss of the child? How much of the loss is alive in "me" now? What do "I" blame for it? Myself? How do "I" relate to extreme poverty? (I experienced it for only a few months in my personal life, but it's still very usable.) I find that Frank Elgin claims "I" was a former Miss America. It puzzles me in relationship to the rest of Georgie's character. Would she ever have been a contestant? Then I realize that Frank has invented this about "me," along with many other lies.

I can examine some of Georgie's characteristic habits now or save them for a later stage of the work. If I ask myself why "I" chew gum all the time, why I have such an aversion to tobacco, why I burn incense in every room wherever I go, I might not find an answer until I had realized that one of my character objectives is cleanliness. "I" chew gum for a clean taste in my mouth. Tobacco is a dirty habit. It stains the fingers and teeth, and fouls the breath. (I might tie it in with Frank's drinking, which I fear as a habit-forming drug.) The incense covers musty odors of tenement rooms, as well as "the restaurant odors downstairs," and sweaty dressing-room smells, the smell of stale liquor.

"My" aversion to Frank's need to be liked and his consequent fawning and hypocrisy is the clue to my created counter-characteristic of stoic directness—*no* buttering up or overingratiating manners.

Every actor should explore similar questions about his role. He should find the questions in the play and solve them for himself with identification. Whether he uses real or imaginary experiences, or both, is unimportant as long as he can believe in them and tap them when he needs them.

This question-and-answer game continues until all possibilities for it are exhausted. To bring about a new me, with new but solid roots, need not be discussed with the playwright, the director, or with fellow actors. It is secret laboratory work, and must stay secret. It is *essential* homework.

23

CIRCUMSTANCES

cir·cum·stance *1. A condition, fact or event determining the occurrence of another fact or event. *2. An essential condition, a primary qualification of a fact or event, an accessory condition. *3. The conditions environing and affecting a person or agent. *4. Accompanying or surrounding detail, especially fullness of detail.

The circumstances given by the author of the play must be dug out of each word he has set down. They can determine or condition our conflicts, can supply our motivations, and specify the nature of our actions. They are rarely dealt with sufficiently. The imagination of the actor can't really begin to work until he has found them, filled them in, rounded them out, and extended them fully. Because of the object-exercises work on the *immediately* preceding circumstances of an event, the conditions of the *present* which surround the event and the expectations of the circumstances for the immediate *future* should be a familiar area of exploration (and work), and hopefully, defining circumstances is already an established work habit. As applied to a play, the obligation to find everything given you by the author in the stage directions about time and place, as well as in the dialogue of the play or hidden underneath the words of the characters, becomes larger and more difficult. Substituting and particularizing is inherent in every aspect of the work. You have to find not just *what* happens, but under what circumstances it happens; what circumstances surround "your" life at home, at work, at leisure, in love and war, what is the state of "your" health and mind before you enter the scene. This will make for an understanding of the immediate circumstances and the influence on the actual events and their inevitability. Circumstances which *change* during the course of the scene must also be taken into consideration as they might make for a change of the objective, and condition the actions (i.e., something burns on the stove while you are serving cocktails to your guests; during an argument with your roommate you are informed that a bill collector is waiting in the next room; during a passionate love scene a storm comes to an end, or a burglar alarm goes off!

The search for past and immediate circumstances has to be made, not only for the beginning of the play but for "your" life during and *between* every act and every scene, unless the action on stage is continuous.

TIME, for the actor, is not just the bluntly stated stage direction of "8 P.M." PLACE means infinitely more than "The drawing room." WHEN and WHERE encompass many elements which the untrained actor often sluffs off or answers superficially. Even extensive notes, considered only factually, will bring about a kind of dry, unusable objectivity. Learning to explore and assess time and place subjectively, making total use of them for the benefit of the role, searching for all of their aspects through the soul and the senses of the new "me" to help bring about a chain of actions is a matter of tenacious, prolonged practice.

When do "I" live? In what century, year, season of that

year, month of the season, week, day, hour, and finally what minute leads me into my first action? These questions must encompass everything *implied* by the century in which "I" live, from the cradle to the grave. The consequences of everything implied by the time are the material out of which I will build "my" life.

What are "my" social concepts, government and laws, religion, fashions, appetites and tastes which come from that time to condition "my" life? Where does something coming from the given year affect me? How does the season influence me? What does the day itself do to me? What is at stake for me in the minute of the day in which my life begins actively to evolve? The more detailed my questions, the more I can hunt for consequent actions and animate them as if they had never been done before. The more I find subjective identification, the more I will believe that "I" am alive in that time. The more sources I have to draw on, the more intuitive "my" responses will be.

Another big question which must be broken down into specifics is, How *much* time do "I" have? Is there time to fulfill my wishes, possibly even to live (if I know I'm dying or in great danger)? Is there time to finish "my" work, to prepare for visitors, to get to bed, to go to the bathroom? *Time* is an active influence on even our smallest daily tasks. Since conflict is at the root of drama (whether comedic or tragic), the playwright often presents us with time pressures, and we must learn to make exact use of them. "I've got time to kill," might also be a force for determining the kind of action.

"*Where* do 'I' live?" is just as large a question as "When?" Before I explore the room where the action takes place, I have to ask in what country, city, village, neighborhood and house "I" live. And I must delve into "my" relationship to all of them. A young man or woman raised in a small New

England village will have been influenced by totally different things from those if he or she had grown up on a sprawling ranch in the far west, or in the slums, or in the elegant section of a large city. A ranch in Australia would exert different influences from one in Arizona, as would a Bavarian village as opposed to one in Maine, or a London slum versus one in Chicago. It *matters* if "your" house is like all the others in the neighborhood, or if it is an elegant old brownstone standing alone among huge office buildings, or perhaps a remnant of better days with tenements right and left of it. The task of making everything particular is just as essential for something which is familiar as for that which is unfamiliar.

Examine your immediate surroundings. If silk, velvet and damask are a part of the room, from whose walls Rembrandts and Titians look back at you while a Bach cantata is being played on a record; if you walk on lush pile carpets and handle leatherbound volumes, pour tea from Meissen porcelain, pull tapestry bellcords to summon servants, and look through Belgian lace curtains at rolling lawns and landscaped gardens—"your" behavior will be powerfully and specifically influenced, and it will be influenced differently whether this is "your" way of life or "you" come to it as a stranger. Now consider that you are surrounded by cracked and peeling walls and ceilings, have wrinkled pop posters pasted to the walls, walk on bare floorboards, and sit on a rickety stool at an oilcloth-covered table in front of a lumpy burlap-covered studio couch, drinking beer from a can to the accompaniment of the Beatles and a leaky faucet, while you look out of the streaked window at a fire escape against a blackened brick wall. If you have truly considered each of these things and made them real to yourself, will "your" behavior (the choice and execution of your action of the dramatic events of the play) be influenced by these things? *Obviously!* There should not be the tiniest thing around you which you have failed to make personal or relate to yourself *if* you want to soar into an exciting new life.

Try now to consider all the previous examples for *Place* (the ranch in Australia, the Bavarian village, the London slum, the room with Rembrandts and the Belgian lace, the room with the pop posters and bare floorboards, etc.), and condition them with *Time*. First try 1850 . . . in a blizzard . . . in February . . . in the middle of the night.

Then 1900 . . . in a heat wave . . . in July . . . at high noon.

Then 1950 . . . on a chilly morning . . . in April . . . at spring's awakening.

Then 1972 . . . in November . . . on election eve . . . during rain.

(Even if the time is "Anytime" or the place is "Limbo," you must create specific realities belonging to it—though you must never create a specific reality which might violate the playwright's time or place.)

The above exercises should make you understand how crucial WHEN and WHERE must become in your preparatory work.

Recently, I found my workbook for the role of Martha (*Who's Afraid of Virginia Woolf?*), and wherever my notes pertain to *Time, Place,* and *Previous Circumstances,* I'll share some of them with you. They are, as I wrote them down, in random order. They may seem a little like Joyce's *Anna Livia Plurabelle.* The names George, Nick, Honey, and Daddy are characters in the play. Of course, Edward Albee wrote the play. All other names belong to my personal life and suggest possible substitutions. The equals (=) sign indicates my use of a substitution. The brackets enclose explanatory notes for you, the reader.

Late *Saturday* night. Late? As a matter of fact, 2 A.M. End of September = crackly red and yellow and brown leaves! *Frosty* night? Hot indoors? Edward means it all to be now. [1962] The new college term just opened. Booze! Football practice? Did I go this afternoon? Who's the coach? = Bradley. Yummy. New semester = faculty teas, heavy drinking at cocktail parties = tension, hysteria from new students, new faculty = the Johnstons, the Garricks, etc.

The party at Daddy's house tonight. A dozen new faculty members. Particularize them! Especially meeting with Nick and Honey = Marian and Dave? Or Marian and Bill? *How* did I show off?—how much to provoke George? Or to impress Daddy? I sang, "Who's Afraid of Virginia Woolf?" I'll bet I read *Orlando* last week! [A novel by V. Woolf] I "brayed." *When?* What about? Boxing? History? Status?

We never discuss politics. Were George and I stung?— Remember McCarthy! [And I don't mean Eugene!] Am I aware of new political movements among young faculty members—like Nick? Or students? Do I try to participate with them? Uh-uh. Cynical, skeptical intellectuals—both George and me. Atheists. Agnostics? = Max and Alicia.

George in the History Department = Art History = Papa's assistants = power plays, like in corporations = also faculty wives jockeying for position = Jack S., maybe Ruth—Oh, yes, yes, yes.

The house is *messy*. Pretentiously unpretentious living! Ugh. Scatter rugs = Prof. Alex's house = Books piled sideways on shelves. Disorder, and = *unwatered* plants. Maybe an instrument lying open? Or the record player? Yes! Hahaha. Open and ready to go. Loose records lying around. The *Eroica?* Or the *Missa Solemnis?* Worn upholstery on "good" furniture. I think it's an *old* house—properly antiqued and comfy. Mortgaged? Is it a "home"? Nope. *Make* the neighborhood = mix together Adams St., Lathrop St., and Walton. *Make* the campus specific = mix up Ithaca, Madison, and Bennington = Faust [Prof. Albert Faust, my uncle].

This town is New Carthage. What was *old* Carthage? I remember some Roman, like Caesar, said, "Carthage must be destroyed!" Edward's symbols? How apt!! Too intellectual for me—can't use it!!! I was born and raised in New Carthage = Wisc. High, maybe Randall school. Grew up in Daddy's—college pres.—mansion = Phil R's house. Did I brag about the mansion? Did I feel lonely there? Did I like somebody else's "home" better? = Jane Mc. Where am I vulnerable to Daddy? When I was little? Now? Vulnerable to George? What areas? Not just *age.*

Make the street = elms, maples, burnt-orange mums—eeek! Neighbors = the W's, they weren't faculty, more conventional. When we come home, George says, "Sssshhh, the neighbors!" Can they hear us making a racket even when we're in the house? During the play?

Make the rest of the house. Have to work on the *bedroom!* The kitchen!—with Nick. The bathroom with Honey! Where do I usually park in the living room? My favorite chair? Are there toys around for our "child"????? Daddy's portrait or photo? Ask Edward if I can use one of Papa. Wow! . . .

24

RELATIONSHIP

re·la'tion·ship *1. Connection; the state of being related.
2. Kinship. *5. The mode in which one thing stands to
another. *6. State of being mutually or reciprocally interested.

AFTER studying the play, you have determined your character's relationship to the theme of the play. You have established your character's relationship to the other characters in
the play in terms of the protagonist and the antagonist: you
have taken sides. Now you have to define the relationships in
detail and bring them into focus from your character's point
of view. Then you have to find substitutions in order to make
your character's viewpoint about the other characters in the
play "your" own!

Once you have understood that the smallest *inanimate*
object on stage must be made particular and personal by
endowing it with the required physical and emotional properties so that even a secondary action dealing with it will have
meaning and pertinence for the character, you will see the
immensity of the task of making particular and real another
human being confronting you. It *is* complex to make the

characters you come in conflict with during your life on stage *actively* real to you! Your aim must be to bring about pertinent *inter*action between yourself and the others.

If you work correctly on your relationships in the play, when your lover touches your cheek, your flesh may tingle as you offer your lips. When your boss fires you, you may get hot under the collar as you inform him that you had already planned to resign. When your son insults you, you might redden with humiliation before putting him in his place. You will shiver with irritation as your girl friend files her nails, until you start singing to drown out the rasping. When you are proposed to, your heart will probably start to pound before you accept. If you have only *assumed* your relationship to the other characters or taken them for granted, you will find only dry, mechanical actions. To find genuine, electrified action you have to endow your relationships with all the elements that constitute a specific relationship and make yourself vulnerable to these elements. Then pit yourself against the other characters, and go!

In almost all human relationships—or at least in certain areas of a relationship—one person dominates and the other submits; one person leads and the other follows. Start with this: Ask yourself how "you" (the character) stand in relation to the other characters. Are you willingly or unwillingly leading or following? Ask yourself in which specific areas. In love? At work? At home? In public? In all of them?

To begin with, define your relationships in broad terms. I love him. I hate her. We are close, like brothers. He's like a parent. We compete like jealous rivals. Is it a relationship of entanglement or indifference? Do you look up to him or down at him? In which areas? Are you afraid of her, or she of you? In which areas? Is the relationship—whether it be one of competition, love, hostility, maneuvering or trading for advantage and position—declared and open, or is it hidden and subconscious? Is it a relationship of pretended closeness with secret distrust? And always ask if it is *reciprocal* or if you are at *opposites*.

Clearly, this broad labeling of basic relationships is founded on circumstances (the length of the relationship and the events which brought you to the present relationship, the way of life—wealth or poverty, work or leisure, the kind of work, etc.) and human needs. The circumstances and needs are based on your character's responsibilities and obligations to the others and his willingness or unwillingness to fulfill them.

Then go further into areas of agreement and disagreement, such as assumptions (right or wrong) which you have about the other characters and which they may have about "you"; your feelings and bias about each other. Explore the past from your first meeting with each other down to the details of your first confrontation. Or, if it is a first meeting in the play, what makes the sparks fly between you (Romeo and Juliet!)?

Then begin the detailed work of examining "your" most intimate likes and dislikes of the others. Do you like or dislike that your lover is a sentimental romantic? Do you enjoy your husband's warring aspects or are you repelled by them? Do you go for his rumpled tweeds and tangy cologne or do they put your teeth on edge? Do you melt when his dimple appears or does it embarrass you? Which of his idiosyncrasies send you and which annoy you? If someone you love shows off in public how does it affect you? (Most people withdraw and become silent, almost antisocial as a result. I used this for Georgie Elgin in *The Country Girl* as she was pitched against her husband. It also works the other way; if you're in a public situation with someone close to you who is antisocial, you compensate by becoming aggressively outgoing.)

Finding identification with the antagonist of the piece

seems to present greater problems for the actor than when he plays the protagonist. The actor often falls into the trap of evaluating the "villain" and pitting him against the "hero" rather than revealing the human being he must play. You must *justify* your character, not judge him, or you will fall into one of two traps. Either you will soften and sentimentalize the character to prove that *"I'm* not really like this," or you will bring about illustrative actions to tell an audience "look how evil *he* is." Because the author has sympathetically justified the behavior of the protagonist it is sometimes difficult for the actor playing the antagonist not to be seduced by this knowledge. To construct a balance between you and the protagonist you have to know *more* about your own needs and *less* about the needs of the others. Otherwise, as antagonist, you will fail in making your relationship to the protagonist through your own character's eyes.

Suppose you are playing the mother in *Look Homeward, Angel,* and you have to throw out your son's true love and tie him to your boardinghouse apron strings, ignoring his sensitivities and artistic needs. You must not identify with *his* problems, but rather, back up the facts for your *own* needs. "You" *do* have to work at least twelve hours a day to keep a roof over his head while dealing with endless, difficult boarders. That girl *is* older and more experienced than he is and may create a burdensome trap for him. He *is* immature and impractical, etc. If you have backed up your needs, when you have to accuse him, or pick on him, or boss him around, you will have justification for your actions and no need to judge them.

Or take the mother in *Butterflies Are Free,* whom the playwright depicts as intruding on her blind son's fight for freedom and independence. The actress, in finding a correct relationship to him, must not forget that he *is* blind, has been undone by a previous love, and might be heading for disaster without his mother's help and supervision. She must evaluate his problems through "her" eyes, not his. The son, on the other hand, often particularizes the relationship to his mother only as an intruding one, and fails to include his love for her, his previous dependence on her; consequently, he omits the obstacle which will make for the genuine actions of his relationship to her.

A relationship can develop and change even *before* we have met up with a stranger. Imagine that I have a script which I ask you to deliver for me. I tell you that I would like you to bring it to Ada Bloom, a literary agent who also handles actors. Her office is on West 56th Street, between Broadway and 7th Avenue. Tell her that I sent you, that you are an actor, and ask if she has any parts for which she might submit you. You will immediately conceive an Ada Bloom in your mind's eye, how she looks, is dressed, speaks, and even how you plan to impress her. You will start speculating on how you will announce yourself. You will visualize the office and its decor. Before you get uptown, your expectations about Miss Bloom, the office, as well as your plan of attack, will have changed at least ten times.

I have invented Miss Bloom. To me she is short and stocky, with cropped hair, and she is wearing a gray serge suit. She is aggressive and hostile. My plan of action is to pounce, and assert myself before she can put me off. Now suppose, as I burst into the office, I am greeted by a tall, round-faced, soft-haired, motherly lady. I have to make speedy readjustments. My expectations change. My attack turns to pussy-footing until I am counteracted by a slight rejection and gentle aloofness. My expectations change again and so does my action. In other words, our relationships to others begin the moment we hear about someone.

Occasionally, the actor mistakenly looks for one person in his personal life to serve as a substitution for his total relationship to a character in a play. It is highly unlikely that he will find a real-life parallel right down the line for all the areas and aspects of the character relationship. It is more likely that he will need aspects of twenty relationships in his life, linked to a variety of experiences in order to create this new relationship in the play. He may need a hundred. For Georgie's relationship to Frank Elgin, I used my father, my child, several crushes and many past loves. As Martha, in order to create the love-hate relationship to George in *Who's Afraid . . .*, I had to isolate *moments* of many relationships in which challenge, vengeance, wounding and vulnerability were at stake. A *composite* of the old will make for the new in relationships.

However thoroughly the actor constructs his relationships to the other characters and however precisely he makes his substitutions, they will not help him a bit if he keeps them in his head. He must use them to receive from, and be vulnerable to, the characters he confronts in order to free the necessary actions. Only when the considered relationships and the substitutions for them lead the actor to actual receiving and then *doing* something, physically and verbally, to the other characters will the results have value.

AGE

The problem of your character's age properly belongs under your considerations for "Who am I?" However, establishing it with faith is so closely linked to your relationships to the other characters in the play that I have reserved it for this chapter.

As our theater is set up, the chance is rare that you will play someone far removed from your own age. In amateur companies, summer stock and drama schools, you will still find the young actor employing the old clichés—the hunched posture, the wobbly head, the cracked voice, and the corn-starched hair—which are supposed to symbolize old age. You will also see the twenty-year-old actor portraying a teenager as if he were a retarded five-year-old, with toes pointed inward, elbows and wrists crooked outward, while lisping his words in a small squeaky voice.

Aside from these obvious technical errors, we have strange notions and misconceptions of age, even in our daily lives. And then we apply these misconceptions to the play, even when the age of our character is within easy range. I knew a twenty-eight-year-old actress who was convinced she was too young to play the forty-year-old Ruth in *Epitaph for George Dillon*. Actually, she only needed to concentrate on the *difference* in age between herself and George Dillon to find a belief in her required age. (In other words, she had to make him about ten years younger than herself.) I also tried to assure her that once having arrived at the ripe old age of forty she wouldn't feel the slightest bit different from the way she did now, nor would she look much different—certainly not across the footlights. To make my point, I also asked her to remember honestly how she felt (or looked) in her late *teens*. Was there a difference? No—although her evaluation of *other* teenagers from her present vantage point might be that they were "just kids!"

There are a few general guideposts to the extremes of age which can be of use. The infirmities which set in with old age come from the fact that *something* is weakening—the joints, the feet, the back, etc. (inner organs don't show). If you *must* play someone who is very old when you are still young, work for a weakness or an ache in one area of your body to bring about an appropriate physicalization (obviously coupled with skillfully executed makeup). It will serve you better than the clichés of old age.

Physically, the "awkwardness" of youth usually stems

from insecurities about social expectations, and an attempt to imitate notions of adult behavior. Sometimes the clothes are too large because they are new, or too small because they are old. Physical and psychological adjustments to clothing, and the relationship to social expectations are essential to dealing with the problem of youth.

Our psychological relationship to others often makes us *feel* that we are younger or older. When I was young, I had a friend who was in his late seventies. He seemed like my contemporary (and I'm sure he felt as though he were) as he joined in with my interests in *now* and in tomorrow. At the same time, I also had a friend in her early forties who seemed like my grandmother as she continuously referred to her age. "I'm so old," she would say, and finish off any argument with, "When you're *my* age you'll know. . . ." She seemed to deal only with the past. Remember that when you were ten, someone who was twenty seemed very adult. At twenty, someone aged forty seemed to be "getting on!" A twenty-year-old is at a ripe old age to himself until he pits himself against a fifty-year-old, who in turn, feels that the other is "just a kid."

What is primarily at stake is that you must find identification with the age of your character. Within yourself you have a rather broad range of years at your disposal. Your character's age will be established by a self-image which may change when placed in relationship to someone older or younger than yourself.

I do a demonstration in class in which I use a student for a partner. The first time I assume that he is Alfred Lunt. We meet and shake hands. I always turn red, and get damp palms, and am on the verge of a bobbing curtsy as our hands meet. In that moment I feel eighteen, inside and out. Then I meet the same student and shake hands, this time assuming he is a rather impertinent friend of my daughter's. I am *tall*, a little condescending and definitely my own age! Occasionally, I add a third handshake with the student and make believe he is Gérard Philipe. No idolotrous teenager confronted with her most worshiped movie star could match my idiotic assault, accompanied by knocking knees.

In your relationship to the other characters in the play, it now becomes obvious that age is a powerful influence. How you deal with the others will spring from your adjustment, among other things, to the fact that you feel they are older or younger than you are; that they merit your respect or are beneath your interest; that they should be coddled because they are younger or older; that they can be sloughed off because they are younger or older. Your related age differences should create specifics in action.

Your adjustments relating to your character's age must, of course, also be aligned to his work, his loves, attachments and appetites, whether they be innocent, knowing, familiar or jaded.

Note that I have not discussed the problem pointed out by the master-technician who claims—usually rightly so—that a young actor may be outwardly the correct age for the part, but that he's not ready to play it in terms of understanding or craft. St. Joan was nineteen when she died. I was thirty-one when I played her. Years later, Dame Sybil Thorndike, who created the role, asked me when I was going to play the part again. I told her I thought I was too old. She replied, "You can only be too *young* for Joan!" Unhappily, the magic of Duse or Ruth Draper, each of whom could transform herself into a young enchantress without covering a silver hair or using makeup, is not only rare but seldom allowed a test in our theater of typecasting.

25

THE OBJECTIVE

ob·jec′tive 1. Pertaining to the object or end. *3. Something aimed at or striven for.

THE ACTIONS of human beings are governed, more than anything else, by what they *want,* consciously or subconsciously. In order to make the hunt for the objectives of the character specific, I divide them into three categories: (1) the overall character objectives; (2) the character's objectives for the individual scenes of the play; (3) the character's moment-to-moment objectives within the scenes.

Certainly, the exploration of the overall objectives is a part of the work on "Who am I?" (No human being *is* without having wants and drives.) Now, in asking, "What do I want?" consciously and subconsciously, and in finding the answers, it becomes evident that I must know more about the character I am going to play than the character knows about himself. (The greater your insight into human needs becomes, the better an actor you will be.) First, ask the questions about character objectives in broad terms. What do I want—in relationship to the world, to my work, to the people in my life? Answers might be: I want to be famous, to make my mark, to be in command, to be needed by others, etc. Or: I want security, a family, protection, to hide from the world, etc. These larger objectives must align themselves with the character's function in the play as protagonist or antagonist, and therefore also serve the objective of the play itself.

If the larger objectives of the character seem alien to me, I look for substitutions as soon as possible. If Medea's need for revenge seems far removed from me—and it *does!*—my remembrance of having been wronged by Joseph McCarthy, and a surging need to get even (although I never acted on this need) can be enough of a springboard for a full psychological identification with the need to revenge myself on Jason.

With the character's overall objectives in mind, the next step is to look for the character's main need or objective for each scene in the play. It should be linked to the events and allow the dramatic conflict to move forward. It should act as a lamp and illuminate the path that must be traveled in the scene. For example, if you need to get across a river, simply *wishing* you were on the other side won't get you there. The need or the wish must light up the possibilities of what to do to fulfill that wish. Will you swim, take a boat, walk on the rocks, or look for a bridge?

These smaller objectives (concerning themselves with the need for a boat—finding oars, bailing out water, wanting to push the boat from the shore—or wanting to locate rocks, testing their slipperiness and size, considering the need to jump from one to another, or wanting to test your prowess against the current or even rapids of the river, or its depth) constitute the *beats* of the scene. A beat begins under a given set of circumstances when an immediate objective sets in. It ends when that objective has succeeded or failed and new circumstances set in.

I heard a delightful but unverified story about the term

beats. Stanislavsky is supposed to have called them "bits," but when explaining them in English with his Russian accent, it sounded like "beats." To me, "bits" fall to pieces. I prefer "beats," which have a pulse as in music. They move ahead, and are connected with something at both ends, with something that has happened and something still to come!

If balancing a conscious objective against a subconscious one poses a riddle in putting it to work, I will give you an example of how I work on it. In Turgenev's *A Month in the Country,* Natalia Petrovna, who is conveniently married to a kind landowner and has a lovely child and an elegant entourage, has main drives (objectives) to have a cultivated and gracious life. She wants to be accepted as an intelligent, generous woman, and she pursues romance in every sense of the word. Her child has a charming young tutor, and without being aware of it, Natalia falls madly in love with him. In a devastating scene with her seventeen-year-old ward, Vera, Natalia tries to make a match between the ward and a fat, old, rich neighbor. Her conscious objective is to provide security and protection for her ward. Her subconscious objective is to get Vera out of the house and away from the tutor because she is jealous of Vera's youth and seeming interest in the tutor. A woman who consciously connives to ruin the life of a young girl would be monstrous and selfish. A woman who does it subconsciously is humanly fallible. There is a point, later in the play, when Natalia's subconscious objective breaks through into her conscious awareness, and her objective becomes to punish herself for her baseness.

(The conscious objective is usually aligned with one's self-image and sense of morality. Consciously, we almost always want to behave well—nobly, with kindness and consideration for others. We sometimes consciously look for *any* justification for ignoble acts into which our subconscious desires may have sent us.)

First, I try to work *openly* on the subconscious needs by looking for all the actions which might spring from them: dealing with Vera as an acknowledged rival—putting her down, challenging her, proving my superiority to her, while allowing her to move in on my senses as a giant irritant. When I have found consequent actions, I bury them and pursue only the actions which have to do with the conscious need to protect her, to ensure her future, to prove my love and kindness to her. The conscious objective is always influenced powerfully by my early work on the subconscious; consequently, I don't have to burden myself with double mental considerations while playing. This is my way of supplying a correct balance. I have observed other actors who have successfully reversed the procedure by working on the conscious objective as their first guide to the actions before making considerations for the subconscious. Mine is simply a personal preference.

If the objectives in all three categories remain factual, and do not set me on a hunt for actions, no matter how true or relevant they may be, I sometimes find the correct stimulus simply by rephrasing. For instance, instead of a need to be alone, I might find that a fight for freedom or a desire to get away from those who burden me is immediately suggestible.

Occasionally, another confusion arises between what you *have* to do and what you *want* to do. Don't confuse an obligation with a desire. Actions which result when I *have* to clean house are totally different from those when I *want* to clean house. Always define your real objectives with wants, needs, desires. What you *have* to do may be an obstacle to what you want.

In the architecture of constructing the character, the objectives are a powerful part of the basic structure. They must be sought out with strong, personal identification if they are to provide a solid foundation for the work on the action.

In summation for the objective let me use, as an example, Shaw's *Saint Joan*.

The objective of the play is clearly stated in Shaw's preface when he emphasizes his need to destroy the sentimental, romantic legend of the wispy, watery-eyed, holy girl by coming to grips with the human facts of the sturdy, strongwilled peasant. Through intense faith, native wit, and a giant sense of right and of herself, she turned France from a satellite into a nation, and pitted herself against the established government and the corrupted church as almost the first nationalist and the first protestor or *protest*ant. An endless variety of broad character objectives present themselves: to serve God; to save France; to do away with lies and weakness; to make a good life for the people of France; to win. Subconscious objectives might concern themselves with a need to prove herself a leader; to prove herself right at any cost; to assert power. There might even be the fulfillment of sensual needs: to give her body to armor, to battle, to the physicality of combat.

As I am personally not a nationalist or religious in a church sense, these objectives might be translated into a need to save the theater, a need to beard the merchants of art in their dens. I might use my admired colleague Fritz Weaver for the Dauphin, and confront him with his ultimate responsibility of assuming his throne in a pure theater. I might force my friend Eli Wallach, instead of Dunois, across the river to battle (instead of the English), the money lenders of the theater and the real-estate owners who have usurped our rights. I might find a powerful objective to serve my art instead of God. Et cetera.

In scene 1 of the play, I need to make a first step, a first conquest. I need to win over De Baudricourt. I want to force him to give me horses and an escort to the court of the Dauphin. In the individual beats, I want to gain entrance; then I want to confront De Baudricourt; I want to bully him; then wheedle him into acquiescence. In the second scene, I need to persuade the Dauphin that he must assert himself, and that he must supply me with an army. In the beats, when I arrive at the Dauphin's court, I must first find *him* (Which one is he among all the courtiers pretending to be him?), and then I need to get him alone, and then I need to find him out as a person, etc.

And I still have one other big job ahead of me before I can start the work on the actions. What's the obstacle? What's in the way of what I want?

26

THE OBSTACLE

ob′sta·cle   *1. That which stands in the way or opposes; a
hindrance, an obstruction to one's progress.

IF I KNOW what I want and can achieve my wishes readily
without any problem, there is no drama. In tragedy and
comedy and satire and farce—in anything that is worthy of
the stage—conflict is at the root. Consequently, finding the
obstacles to my objectives becomes imperative. I have to look
for the crisis, the conflict, the clash of wills—the drama.

What's in the way of what I want? Who's against me?
What's against me? Pose these questions against your character objectives, against your main objectives, and against your
immediate objectives in the beats of the scenes. Your needs
should strengthen in the desire to overcome the obstacles.
Remember the old adage that something difficult to obtain is
always more strongly desired than something readily available. The obstacle itself will strongly influence what you
must *do* to overcome it in the pursuit of the objective.

There are obstacles within the overall character objectives. For example, I want to become a great artist. I want to

maintain high ideals. I want to avoid the tawdry and the commercial aspects of art. (How many of you have a passionate objective to make your mark in the theater, but balk at the ugly aspects of making the "rounds"?) Suppose your main objective in the scene is to win the part at the audition, *but* your competitor is your best friend. In the immediate objective of the first beat, you want to fix yourself up to look right for the part, but your mirror is broken. Can you borrow one from your best friend? Your competitor?

Obstacles will be inherent in, or spring from any element of, the given material: from the character itself; from something in the past and present circumstances; from the relationships and opposing objectives of the other characters; from the events; from the surroundings; and from the objects themselves.

Here is a simple example of selections for the obstacle. You want to set the table for important guests. First, try to set the table without an obstacle, while you are observed, to discover how you have to fight for concentration, and how time drags, and how involvement becomes a major problem. Then test your objective against an *obstacle* coming from:

1. *Character:* You are a perfectionist, but you are fearful of failure. Now try to set a *perfect* table.
2. *Your past:* You have had a pampered life surrounded by servants, and have never set a table before. Or you come from a slum and have only recently joined the middle class. You aren't certain of the proper placement of flatware, dishes, glasses and napkins.
3. *Time:* You have only five minutes in which to do it.
4. *The objects:* The dishes are elegant and borrowed. Or they are chipped, cheap, don't match, or there aren't enough to go around.

5. *Circumstances:* Your husband is asleep in the next room. The dinner is a surprise, and you don't want him to hear you.

6. *The relationship:* The guests are your husband's employers or relatives. They are very fussy, and you need to impress them.

7. *Place:* The room is small, and the table hasn't enough space for the number of settings you require.

8. *Weather:* There's a heat wave or a cold snap. No air-conditioner. Broken furnace.

9. Et cetera.

Try setting the table using these obstacles. Watch what happens!

In the attempt to overcome the obstacle the nature of the actions starts to become evident, and in the struggle to overcome it your will should strengthen. If the door you want to open is stuck, your temperature rises!

Actors continuously ask, "But is there *always* an obstacle?" Yes! Obviously, the obstacle must always be logical to the character in the given circumstances. I'm not recommending that you hunt for a score that will match *The Perils of Pauline*. But if the obstacle isn't inherently clear to you, you'd better find one!

I have another favorite demonstration. My circumstances are seemingly ideal. My lover has just proposed. He's rich. We have all interests in common. Our parents adore the idea that we are getting married. The minister is available. The weather is great. We both look gorgeous. No obstacle! The director says, "Jump up in the air for joy." I do. I feel like a fool. *Then* I decide that gravity is my obstacle, that I want to jump up, but can't get as high as I want. I *leap* up and push against gravity, and my heart begins to pound and I laugh aloud with delight!

The Obstacle

Even if you are a character who has to *sleep* during the play, you can establish an obstacle. Explore the lumpy mattress, the narrowness of the bed, the hardness of the pillow or—"To sleep, perchance to *dream*. Ay, there's the rub!"

27

THE ACTION

ac'tion   *1. The doing of something; being in motion or operation. 2. An act done. *3. Behavior, conduct. *4. The influence or effect of something on something else. 5. An event or series of events, real or imagined, forming the subject of a play.

OCCASIONALLY, after doing all the other preparatory work, an actor still doesn't seem to understand what a real action is. It is *not* "stage business" or being "busy," or posing physically, or setting words with mechanical inflections, or illustrating verbal ideas, or making mechanical "shapes" for the stage life of the character. Nor is an action an illustration of an attitude or a mood. Nor is acting "*re*acting," as so many old pros insist.

"Acting" is *doing! Everything* I have dealt with up to this point should lead to action. Even the object exercises and their specific technical problems should have served you in the discovery of the awareness of genuine action. All of the homework and the rehearsal work for the exploration of the play, the work on sense memory, the hunt for the character and identification through substitutions, the search for the circumstances, the relationships, the objectives and obstacles *must have their consequence in actions* or nothing has been of value. The sum total of the actions (what you *do* from moment to moment) reveals your character. The selection of the actions must tell the story of the body and soul of your character, the new "you"! Your selection and execution will also be the determining factor of the degree of your artistry.

I have assiduously avoided the word *attitude* throughout this book, not because human beings don't have them, but because actors so often confuse attitudes with actions, or put them in, in the place of actions. The misguided actor predetermines an attitude toward a given person, object, circumstance or event; he even finds an objective and then rides or floats toward it with his "attitude." He mistakenly thinks he is in action. Instead of the word *"attitude,"* I have deliberately used words such as *particularizations, likes, dislikes* and *adjustments* to the person, the object, the circumstance, the relationship, etc. If you find particular adjustments to these elements and load them for yourself, they will condition the *nature* of the action which should be operative in overcoming the obstacles and get you to your objective.

You can strike the word *attitude* from your vocabulary because it can't be played. I get so single-minded about this misunderstanding that I recommend my own way of avoiding the danger. I first retype the script to eliminate *any* adjectives of the stage direction. Or, at my first reading of the play, I cross them out so heavily that I can't possibly see them. "Angrily," "sadly," "gloomily," "gladly," "smilingly," "passionately," "shyly," etc., do not belong in *anybody's* acting score. They are *not* actions! If you should happen to smile or frown or feel sad or glad or furious or frustrated or shy or loving, it will be a *result* of your particularizations for each object, person, event or circumstance—and the result of the give and take of the actions! If you select adjectives as a part of your acting score, you will simply make faces, strike poses, and guarantee that you *won't* be in action!

Shakespeare gives the actor no adjectives. Goody! In contemporary plays it is a different matter. When the printed version of *The Country Girl* came out there were even more descriptions than in the original manuscript. I asked Clifford Odets about this. He explained that the original script was not intended for the actors but for the financial backers of the production. As most of them were unimaginative and didn't really know how to read a play, he put in the descriptions for them. He said that the hard-cover version was for just plain readers, not doers. He inserted pages of description which he took directly from the final, staged production. One example fascinated me in particular. During a rehearsal of a fight scene between my husband, Frank Elgin, and myself, when I was threatening to walk out on him, I reached for my coat. By accident, the sleeve was inside out, and I had a big struggle with it. It helped the action of the scene for me so I asked the stage manager (who had to preset the coat on stage) to make certain that the sleeve was always inverted. In the printed text of the play Clifford Odets had a description of Georgie snatching her coat from the chair, struggling with the sleeve, turning red with suppressed rage, yanking the coat over her shoulder, fighting back tears while accusing Frank of having lied and humiliated her, etc. Why in the world should another actress be asked to repeat either the adjectives *or* the sleeve when she might come up with something of her own? Cross out these descriptions, and let your own sense of character guide you. An experienced actor learns to read the play for the human intentions, without the descriptions.

Settling for the "mood" is as dangerous as going for an attitude. Spelled backwards, it is *doom* for the actor. A mood *results* from the sum total of the actions. But trying to "get into the mood" or playing it can only lead to mush!

The Action

Discovering a *real* action, a *real* doing, is the continuous and constant work on the part. "What do I do to get what I want?" "How do I get what I want?" (By doing what?) "What do I do to overcome the obstacles, and how do I overcome them?" (By doing what?) Look for active verbs!

(Many actors and teachers reject the word *how* because they believe it leads to adjectives rather than actions. Grammatically, *how* is an adverb. My favorite, Mr. Webster, defines *how* this way: "1. By what means? 2. For what purpose? 3. To what effect?" My *means, purpose,* or *to what effect* cannot be answered by *gladly,* by *smilingly,* or by *angrily!*)

The cold might make me *reach* for a sweater or a coat; the rain might make me *duck* or *open* an umbrella; the heat might make me *mop* my brow or *take off* my blouse; the quiet might make me *tiptoe* or *skirt* the squeaking floorboards; the time might make me *start running;* old age might make me *limp* or *cover* my wrinkles or *dye* my hair; my youth might make me *don* high heels; a mouse might make me *jump;* an enemy might lead me to *challenge* him; an insult might make me *fight;* my fear might make me *hide*—if it so fits. Otherwise, all of these considerations have been for nothing. To get someone's attention, you can *stare* or *fix* on him (not just *shout* at him) so intently with your eyes that he must look back at you. To win someone over, you can *butter* him *up, break down* his defenses, *stroke* him, *bully* him, etc. These are primitive examples, but they should clarify how you must be propelled into action, into the animation of body and words. My old friend, the cat, following the lint with its eyes and considering whether or not to pounce, is in powerful action even before the actual pounce.

Really doing something is quite different from mechanically doing it, or simply clicking off mentally that you're doing it, or showing the audience that you're doing it. When you are *really* in action, you are engrossed in the action and alert to its possible effect on the object toward which the action is directed. In the execution of the action, you are not seeing or listening to yourself, you are not watching "how." You should leave yourself wide open—with expectations—as to what the result of the action will be. Will it succeed or fail? What will be done back to you by the person or object which will then propel you into the next doing?

I like to make a comparison between a sporting event such as fencing, Ping-Pong, tennis or boxing, and an acting scene. In your athletic contest, if you watch your wrist or fingers, or stance, or your own lunge, or how prettily you serve, neither your foil, ball or fist will reach its mark. If you watch yourself *after* lunging or sending the ball or the fist, your opponent will catch you off-guard or stab you to death. Curtain!—for the athlete and the actor long before the end of the play.

The fulfillment of your character's wishes juxtaposed against the circumstances and the other characters' wishes entails real sending and receiving. Cause and effect, receiving and doing something about what you receive in response to an assumption, or an imaginary stimulus—this is what acting is all about.

Actions, from the largest to the smallest, can be defined and divided exactly as they have been divided into the three categories for the objectives and the obstacles: overall character actions to overcome overall obstacles in order to fulfill overall objectives; the main action to overcome the main obstacle and achieve the main objective; and finally, the immediate action to overcome the immediate obstacle and fulfill the objective within the individual beats of the scene.

Always work positively. Don't search for what the character *won't* or *wouldn't* do, but what he *might* or *must* do. Test the action by seeing if it really gets you where you want. Only dismiss it if it has no before and after. Then look for another one.

Here are some possible examples based on Lyubov Andreyevna in Chekhov's *The Cherry Orchard.*

Overall character objectives [obstacles] and overall actions

1. I want to hang onto the past. (The society is changing.) I will clutch at and grapple with all romantic memories. I will turn memories into tangibles.

2. I want to keep my home and the cherry orchard. (They are mortgaged. I am deeply in debt.) I will try to woo and win over creditors and prospective buyers, pull rank. I will shut out the crumbling and cracking, and turn it back into a romantic "estate."

3. I want to fight every unpleasant reality. (Bickering servants. Miserable, lonely poor relations. Endless responsibilities.) I will deal through a veil with my loved ones and make ideal promises to one and all. I will shut out and ignore and tear up all practical obstacles as though they did not exist.

4. I need my lover. (He's in Paris, the relationship is teetering. He's on the run. He borrows from me, uses me.) I will work hard to delude myself. I will romanticize the best in him. I will write, pursue him, make him need me.

5. I want to be an ideal woman and mother. (I am selfish, need to assert my own needs, need the attention and admiration of my child and all around me. I want them to accommodate themselves to my needs.) I will hug and hold and give and pamper—and demand.

6. I want to delay all goodbyes. (Everyone and everything is changing, aging, leaving.) I will hang on.

Scene One. Main objectives [obstacles] and actions of the homecoming.

To reaffirm my memories. I want to bring back the last time. I want to cope ideally with the changes and shut out the obstacles. (I've traveled for days with little sleep. It's dawn. Everyone else is tired, some are irritable, some hysterically overpowering. The room, my nursery is changed around. A nouveau-riche peasant neighbor is waiting, etc.) My main actions might be to beg for recognition, to make myself ideal in their eyes, to clutch, to stroke, to reach out for tenderness and comfort.

THE FIRST BEAT. I want to get *in*—the nursery. (The dogs are barking, everyone is making noise, storming in on me.) I will touch on and drink in every object, every memory connected with it—sensorily. I will look for comfort—for my orchard—etc.

The selection of the actions is like an orchestration for the theme. The individual actions are like the notes which make up the beats. The beats make up the phrase, the phrases complete the movement, and the movements make up the symphony.

My greatest theater memories are of the unforgettable *actions* of the great actors. What stayed with me was not so much that their actions were theatrically "effective," but that they were overpoweringly selective in revealing to me something about a human being. In Duse's film, *Ashes,* her confrontation with her grown son after she has become a prostitute and is destitute leads her to a deep bow before him, her head almost touching the ground in deep shame and self-abasement which asks for his forgiveness. Even on the *recording* of John Barrymore's *Hamlet* it isn't just his active shriek of "Vengeance!" which one remembers, but the sound of *the action* of his ripping the king's cloak in half!

28

THE REHEARSAL

In English, the word *rehearsal,* derives from a rehearing. In French, rehearsal is *la repetition,* and it means what it sounds like—a repetition. My favorite meaning comes from the German *die Probe* which sounds like what a rehearsal ought to be: the probe! I want to probe, to test, to try . . . to adventure!

Rehearsing or probing entails some fundamental principles which bear examination. The first has to do with ethical behavior. Be good colleagues! Be professional in the best sense of the word. *Never* tell each other what to do or what not to do. Make yourself responsible for serving the play and your colleagues, but don't make them responsible for being at *your* service. Remember that egomania has been one of the chief causes of something being rotten in the state of the theater. Don't let yourself be a part of that.

Be *punctual* or early to every rehearsal. Respect each other's valuable time. There are no excuses for tardiness, short of death or natural disasters. Come *prepared* to each rehearsal. Don't expect others to do your work for you! Stop socializing! Most actors peter away half their lives "getting to know each other" ("When I played . . . ," "This agent told me that . . . ," "Did you read the reviews of . . . ," "My parents think I'm wasting my time in the theater. . . .") You *are* wasting it, if you spend your rehearsal time in this way! Get to know each other through your *work!* If a rehearsal is in your own home, and you feel compelled to serve coffee, have it ready, offer it quickly—and get to work!

Let me deal first with the rehearsal problems which arise for the actor when he is preparing a scene for studio presentation, where his audience will consist of his teacher and his fellow acting students. (As a teacher, my work centers on criticizing prepared exercises and scenes. The scenes have been assigned and rehearsed by the actors, without the presence of a director, for the purpose of developing their craft.) Presenting scenes in class and receiving criticism without the pressures imposed by the final communication of a finished performance before a paying audience should help to exercise the actor's craft through the glorious freedom to fail, the daring to try and to risk. Having to play safe stunts the growth of any artist.

Occasionally, an actor will feel a different kind of pressure in a studio, because, in essence, he is under a microscope. His colleagues and his teacher *know* what he's up to—certainly more than an audience who has the right to know nothing, technically. (When I am performing and am aware that there are students in the audience, I'm being tested far more severely than I am by the critics because the students know more. How can I knowingly cheat technically on stage or violate the goals I hold up to them in class every day?)

I usually assign a particular scene to two actors *in class,* so that even *before* they meet for their first rehearsal they will have had the opportunity to study the whole play individually, and have done a considerable amount of homework on their character's past and private life, and have made substitutions and particularizations for all the things which might influence their character up to the beginning of the scene.

At their first "probe," I recommend reading through the scene together once or twice for content only. Don't try to *act* it, because you can't possibly know *how* and *what* to act yet, and don't try to impress each other with what fine actors you are. Read the scene aloud, for what it's about, and for what's at stake, so you can hear each other. Look at each other. Examine the meaning as you go and *avoid* "line readings" and "emotions"!

Great damage can be done at a first reading by loudly emoting, overshooting the mark, or gentle mumbling. (Have you ever noticed that a gently mumbling actor is usually indicating and coloring the lines just as much as if he were overprojecting, except that he believes if it is *quiet* neither he nor you will notice it?)

After the first or second reading, the actors usually feel impelled into a discussion. Don't! Or keep it to a bare minimum. Beware of essays, intellectualizing and fancy theorizing. Don't talk—*do!* If your characters have known each other in the past, set up some improvisations on your past life together. If your characters are competitive, a few hands of rummy or a game of checkers trying to beat each other will cover more than ten hours of talk. If the scene is a crisis between man and wife, occurring when he comes home from work, improvise a normal homecoming, doing all the things you might do together when he comes home on a routine day. Then see how the crisis alters the behavior. Also improvise on previous circumstances, together or separately, depending on the play. Et cetera.

Instead of discussing the place where your scene occurs, get on your feet and start to set it up. Otherwise, you will each fantasize and discuss the room, the meadow or kitchen for ten hours and probably disagree, sticking to your own imagined place. Or if you should agree, when you finally arrive at tangibly constructing the place, it will end up unrelated to your fantasies. Move the furniture around to make your new "place." Move it again and again. Don't settle immediately. Build your place for your game of make-believe.

If the scene occurs in your character's room, and your partner is the visitor, let him pump you about every aspect of it as you set it up—or vice versa. Don't worry only about the placement of the chair, table and couch, but examine what should be on them, what's around them, their texture, their content. Sit on everything, touch everything, walk everywhere, look everywhere (even though you may not sit on, walk on, touch or look at all of it in the scene). Ask not only about a window, but what's around it and in front of it, and what you can see through it. What books, rugs, magazines, pictures, vases and other objects are there? Endow and make particular the things that are there for the service of the scene. Even if your eyes only touch on an object for a fleeting second in the final work, it will have been worth it. Don't make "stage" decisions about when you will use what or for what purpose. Decisions will come later.

When you consider the circumstances of time, weather, state of health and being, *do* something about them. For instance, if it is supposed to be an overheated (or chilly) room, work for a sense memory and see what happens as you explore and handle the objects in the room. In other words, wherever you can *do* instead of *talk,* do so!

When I insist that you don't tell each other what to do, I mean not only the obvious ("Look at me on that line," "Why don't you walk around a little more?" "It would help if you were a little more threatening," etc.) I mean literally never tell, advise or "help" your partner with his role! You immediately become a director instead of an actor. You also become his audience by watching him and judging whether he's more threatening to you, or walking around enough, or looking at you on cue. You destroy all innocence of receiving.

If the information or the facts of the scene are unclear, you obviously must come to an agreement about them. But don't verbalize your *wishes* or your *actions* or your *obstacles,* or theorize about them. You will immediately become self-conscious and destroy the confrontation with your partner, and the possibility for true interaction!

I can make some funny examples, taken from my own experiences, for how to avoid "your fault" talk. If the other character is supposed to stop you from leaving the room, but doesn't do it quickly enough—leave! The next time that actor will stop you on time. You never have to say, "You're supposed to stop me there," or "You didn't say your line fast enough." It also works in reverse. If the other actor rushes out and leaves you no room for your line, let him. Don't say, "You're not giving me enough time for my line." If the other actor is off circumstances, instead of arguing, go along with him, and the scene will grind to a halt for him. Use what the other actor does, make his signals alive by endowing them with what you need and want.

After conceiving and exploring the previous circumstances and everything tangible in the place, put the first beat of the scene on its feet. If you have worked for several hours on the place (for a five-minute scene) and have thoroughly examined the objects which surround you, it won't be time wasted. If you work several more hours on the first beat of the scene, it won't be too much time spent either.

Suppose you are playing the first scene of Ibsen's *A Doll's House,* and you are doing the part of Nora. Imagine the amount of work you can put in on discovering everything you, Nora, have been doing in the parlor preparing for

Christmas, before your partner, Christine, is announced and how you deal with the recognition of Christine in the first thirty seconds after her entrance. Or if you are playing Christine, there is an enormous amount of work in exploring how you get into the house and in preparing yourself for your first meeting with Nora after a long separation, with such high stakes involved in trying to get what you need from her. This first beat can be improvised, tried, tested and "probed" for a long time to make certain the circumstances, the previous relationship, the objectives and obstacles are operative.

Not one piece of "blocking" will be necessary because your physical life will organically evolve from all the things you have just tested. Not one line will have to be memorized or fixed because the volition which will send you into the verbal actions will have sprung from your character's needs. When the first beat seems to be valid and the accompanying words have run out, pick up the script and continue to the next beat. If the seemingly endless work on that first beat has been solid, the next one should evolve and the work will become less agonizing.

Avoid run-throughs at all costs. Save them for the last. And don't finish a rehearsal just because it "felt good" or was "comfortable." If your inner and outer sources were vague, your place and objects and objectives general, your action work will be fuzzy. So no matter how good it "felt," unless that one-in-a-million moment of inspiration blows your way, the next *running through* will be full of hot air.

When the scene is ready for studio presentation (after you have incorporated all the elements necessary and executed them to the best of your ability), you may still have problems which you don't know how to solve. But that's why you are testing your work for your teacher and colleagues. If you present the scene for "applause" you are working incorrectly. You will have been objectively editing and directing. The most valuable criticism you get will involve the areas where you have failed in *subjectivity*. This occurs whenever you have stalemated your innocence, where, whatever objective work you may have had to do, failed to free your intuitions, failed to lead you to an acting score which could be executed *spontaneously* with all the logic of your character in action. Whether or not your concept for the material is ideal, whether or not you are upstaging or being upstaged, whether or not the mechanical trappings of the scene function is all immaterial for scene study.

The same holds true if you are observing your other colleagues' scene work and listening to the criticism they are receiving. Avoid becoming an "audience." Don't judge, don't approve or disapprove. Concern yourself with their technical problems and *identify* with them. If the work is successful, ask yourself why. If it is unsuccessful in certain areas, ask yourself why. See if you can use the criticism the other actors receive to relate to your own problems, where yours are similar. We are always most open-minded and understanding when our problems are discussed in terms of someone else. Sometimes we learn most off the backs of others. Adulation or putting-down, approval or disapproval, is just opinion, bunkum and gossip.

When you are rehearsing in a professional production, all the ethical principles I have shouted about are equally valid, with one major addition—respect for your director! You must have a willingness to understand and deal with his ideas and concept of the play, and acknowledge his final authority. He is an exact counterpart to the conductor of an orchestra. You are a member of his orchestra, and even if you are the soloist of a concerto, you'd better not take off on your own without him. If the first or the last fiddle, the timpani or horn, the flute or oboe takes off with his own interpretation, the result will be not only anarchy, but such a schmier, such a mishmash that the audience will run away in horror! That happens a lot in the theater, on and off Broadway, in the provinces and capitals of our country.

The director's concept must be followed, and your job is to make it live. It is your job to justify, make throb, and make exist that which he asks of you, whether you agree or not. You must be flexible enough to go *with* him.

Many "modern" actors are ignorant of the fact that Stanislavsky himself gave demonstrations of actions, and very precise line readings when he was directing. The actor was *expected* to make them organically into his own. I once did a play with George Abbott. All our friends thought that the difference in our working methods would produce chaos. During the first week of rehearsal he gave me every inflection for every word of my role, and as we got on our feet he demonstrated every gesture for me. I felt constricted and miserable. I didn't argue because I don't believe in anarchy, but finally, in a wild moment of frustration, I imitated him *exactly*. He stopped me short with, "Don't *copy* me! Don't you know what I *mean* when I show you what to do?" Once I understood that he was giving me intentions, we sailed along and had a marvelous time working *together*.

Many directors talk at great length about the play and the characters and the objectives. Never shut your ears, but avoid letting what you hear lead you to intellectualizing rather than freeing your senses and being stimulated to doings.

There's a lovely story about the great German director Max Reinhardt. An actor was talking on and on about what he'd rather do in the scene. Reinhardt stopped him and said, "Don't tell me. Show me!"

Over and over again, I also have heard actors arguing about something the director was asking them to do, but when the director obligingly asked, "What would you rather

do?" there was silence or hemming and hawing. So—listen!
Work like a dog! Justify! Make everything internally real to
yourself! Serve the playwright, the director, your fellow
actors and consequently the audience!

Let me end with a story I find both funny and pertinent.
Boris Aronson, the famous stage designer, once said in his
mellow Russian accent: "I don't understand Broadway. The
director says he will direct against the play, that I should
design against the play. The actors say they will play against
the lines. If they are all so against it, why are they doing
it?"

29

PRACTICAL PROBLEMS

Ten times each week I am asked the same questions. "How can I become a great artist?" "What do I do about nerves?" "What do I do to get an audition?" "How do I get a job?" "Won't I get bad habits in summer stock or dinner theaters?" "Do you think I'm talented?" "Should I try to stick it out in the theater?" "Am I as good as Duse?" "How do I keep fresh in a long run?" Etc., etc., etc.

Let me try to answer the answerable.

PERFORMER'S NERVES

Very often, the young actor asks me or informs me about *using* his nerves for the character in the given circumstances. To me, this is like using real nausea for the moment when the character is supposed to be nauseated on stage. It can only lead to further lack of control and possibly to disaster.

Or they ask me how to "talk" themselves out of nerves. Once I actually succeeded in doing this for a Broadway opening by telling myself that the entire event was ridiculous and didn't matter, and that everyone in the audience was a dope.

I might as well have stayed home, and I got deservedly bad reviews. Personally, my nerves, just as in the old adage, have increased with experience—or age—and I have come to accept them the way an older athlete might. At best, I hope they will heighten my energy and make me more alert. They should *not* make for fear. Above all, I try to control them by focusing on my main objects and intentions, using my technique to keep me in the universe of the play.

An acrobat will not only get nervous but fall from the tightrope if he looks down, tries to show off, or questions his sense of balance instead of trusting his technique and concentrating fully on his task. An actor's nerves can similarly put him out of commission if he shows off or if his acting score is general, has been thrown together quickly or his preparation is shoddy.

When you are beginning to learn a correct technique, as your goals get higher and you become more aware of the areas in which you might fail, you also may be, temporarily, more nervous than when you proceeded with the faith of an unknowing beginner. Just remember that the better your technique becomes, the more you should be able to concentrate, to eliminate distractions and shed the concerns of your private life in order to involve yourself in the life of your character. Don't replace the joy of playing (or making love) with the nerves which result from a personal ambition for success.

"HOW DO I GET A JOB?"

"Do the rounds" of agents, producers, directors for off-off, off, and on Broadway, for regional theaters, for summer stock, for dinner theaters. Do the rounds over and over again until the soles of your shoes are worn thin. In order to do them and to face everyone, develop a thick skin. (Keep your thin skin and your sensitivities for the work on the character.) Be as prepared in your craft as is humanly possible. Keep practicing forever. Be prepared with audition material. Have thirty things ready to be presented at the drop of a hat. Have material ready for *any* audition, whether it be for a soap opera at a television office or for a classic in New York or the provinces. Have monologues ready, and prepare scenes with obliging partners who can assist you when you need them. (It will probably be to their benefit to help you, if *you* have arranged for the audition.) I have seen actors lose work again and again because after reading something for a director, producer or agent, upon being asked, "What else can you show me?" the answer was, "Nothing."

AUDITIONS

How you land an audition in order to get a job must be separated from how you work on a part. When you apply for an interview, a job, an audition to get the job, you are in point of fact selling yourself in much the same way that a Fuller Brush man sells his merchandise. How you manage it is your individual problem. If you are sensible, you can learn to protect yourself from any element you might meet up with in the theater, except criminality, and for that you should go to the police. Or to Actors Equity Association, your trade union, which is there to protect you. The producer, the agent, the director for whom you want to audition has the same power as the housewife who might slam the door in the face of the brush salesman, or who might let you inside to show your wares.

Auditions can range from an open call where the actors are lined up across the stage like cattle and are eliminated—without a reading—because they are too tall or short, fat or thin, fair or dark, or lately, because they are the wrong astrological sign, to a situation in which you are given time to study the script, work on the scene, and have an opportunity to present yourself at your best. There is also my favorite kind of audition, in which you may present material of your own choosing which you have prepared in advance.

What you should do at a reading, even a cold reading for which you have been given little or no time to prepare, is to go out on a limb: give yourself an objective and then head for it with improvised actions which are as real as possible. Try for a full performance with your improvised actions. Endow *whoever* might read with you into the living substance which could serve you. Your craft will serve you, if you have a craft. Even a mediocre director will hold you because of your *reality,* not on your interpretation. A director wants what any primitive audience wants—to believe that you *are,* to believe that you are really saying what you read from the script.

Remember: Whoever may employ you is totally disinterested in your credos, so don't burden them with that.

"DO YOU THINK I HAVE TALENT?"

To quote Max Reinhardt: "Never mind your talent! Do you have tenacity?" Or, to quote my mother: "Talent is a gift which *many* people have. What you make of it determines whether or not you will be an artist!"

"HOW CAN I WORK CORRECTLY IN SUMMER STOCK?"

With only a week's rehearsal you have to set yourself different goals. A painter can make a very fine quick sketch which people enjoy looking at. He doesn't ask that it be considered a finished oil painting. Very often, long before the stock season has begun, and you have signed your contract, you may already know which plays and parts are to be yours. Here is where I have found actors to be unbelievably lazy, really missing their chance, when they don't immediately set about their homework.

In stock, your speed and flexibility will be marvelously tested. Also, the experience of performing for an audience cannot be replaced by refusing jobs for fear of getting bad habits. Whatever damage you do to your instrument by having to produce quick results can be corrected afterward.

"SHOULD I STICK IT OUT IN THE THEATER?"

If you have to ask this question—*don't!*

WHAT ABOUT THE PACING? THE RHYTHM? THE TEMPO?

These questions fall into the same category as "louder, faster, funnier!" or the "mood." They all spell *doom* if you, the actor, concern yourself with them. They are now, always have been, and always will be the results of the actions, how you head for your objectives under the correctly defined circumstances. The responsibility for these results is in the hands of the director.

"DO YOU THINK I WAS OVERACTING?"

There is no such thing as over or under. There is only *acting.* No moment is too big or too small if it has validity for the moment in the play. Overacting, as it is usually thought of, means that the actor is playing to the gallery instead of with the other characters on stage. Or that he is hanging onto his own sensations or wallowing in false emotion. Underacting is primarily an empty imitation of nature, the actor playing in the "manner" of naturalness, unrelated to the roots of the given *reality*.

"HOW DO I STAY FRESH IN A LONG RUN?"

I think I am one of the few actors in the world who *loves* long runs. The challenge to make a character live anew, as if for the first time, as if never before, night after night after night, is, to me, almost more exciting than the idea of playing in repertory. Several times I have been lucky enough to run as long as two years in a good part in a good play, and each time I have found something brand new internally at the closing performance which I deeply regretted being unable to put to use the next night. I have found that something gets stale or dries up *only* when I become aware of outer effects or of *watching* my actions rather than staying involved and truly executing them. The two-year run can help you to deepen, and to *be* the character for those few hours every night. It has also fascinated me how work which I had done, perhaps a month before I began official rehearsals, seemed to emerge from my subconscious maybe a year later to add a new or different dimension to my character. Sometimes I've longed to play at least six months in front of an audience before any critic would come to see me.

"HOW DO I WORK WITH A REPLACEMENT IN THE CAST?"

If, after a play has been running, an actor leaves the company and is replaced by a new actor, I find it as challenging to work with the new actor as I do running for a long time with the same actor. *I* have also been a replacement on a number of occasions and often suffered from the treatment of bored actors who didn't want to change or adjust their performances to mine, or to change their daily routines to come to "new" rehearsals. As a result, I have lived up to a vow never to put another actor into this spot, and have worked as diligently with a new replacement as though the play were brand new to me.

It should be exhilarating, not tedious, to go along with the ideas of a new partner, unless you treat the theater as just a place to check in and out of. It's a sure proof of working inaccurately if your performance *doesn't* change with a different actor. Your *opinion* about liking the new actor more or less than the first actor is irrelevant!

An extraordinary experience occurred while I was playing Blanche. While the four principals of the New York company took a summer vacation, they were replaced by the four of us who were to go on tour as the National company. Jessica Tandy took off six deserved weeks of rest, and the other three took only two weeks. This meant that I would work first with the National company—Anthony Quinn, Mary Welch, and Russell Hardie—and then—*two* weeks later —with Marlon Brando, Karl Malden, and Kim Hunter. I got in a few rehearsals with the New York company before playing with them, except for Marlon! For a number of reasons, he didn't appear backstage until thirty minutes before we were to go on stage for an SRO performance. We had *never* seen each other's performance. Miss Tandy's and my interpretation of Blanche were as different as Mr. Quinn's and Mr. Brando's Stanley. There was a hasty conference backstage: Should we risk playing together without a single rehearsal and without any knowledge of each other's interpretation? Tony, who was standing by in full makeup, said he hoped Marlon would play because he didn't want to hear the groans of disappointment from the audience if they were told Marlon wasn't playing. Finally, I said, "Let's try to rehearse the first five minutes of the play and see what happens." It was such an adventure that we were both game, and on we went. *Nothing* went wrong, and a lot went right. What made it work? Both of us were totally familiar with place, objects, and circumstances. Neither of us was willful or selfish. Neither of us violated the intentions of our characters. The rest of the four weeks continued to be adventurous. And so was returning to Anthony Quinn.

"HOW DO I TALK TO THE AUDIENCE?"

Whether I am talking to the audience in a Shakespearean play, a Molière, in *The Matchmaker, The Glass Menagerie, Joe Egg,* or *The Bald Soprano,* specific principles always apply. I am not talking to myself; the audience is my *partner!* This partner, the audience, must be made as particular as any other character with whom I have a dialogue in the play. *Who* are they? What's my relationship to them? *Where* are they—in time as well as place? *Why* are they there, what is the obstacle, and *what* do I want from them? Answering these questions, I stand a good chance of finding my actions with them.

Whether I'm talking to one person or to many, I specify my relationship to them—are they with me or against me, do we have a past together, or are we new to each other, etc.? I always put my audience into the time and place in which the play unfolds. I might use courtiers sitting in the king's loge, contemporaries of Molière, if I'm working on a play of his and asked to address the audience. Or I might take some friends from Yonkers at the turn of century who are listening to me and watching me from another sitting room or from the street, if I'm talking to the audience as Mrs. Levi in *The Matchmaker.* Or I might address the audience as if they were specific people coming out of the pub into the street if I, as Launce, in *The Two Gentlemen of Verona,* am lamenting to them about my poor dog, etc. I don't want to have to hurdle the realities I've created in the play for time and place by having to use the audience in the theater on 45th Street in 1973 as is. The faith in my very sense of *being* the character would be shaken.

Now comes the hardest part! You want your audience to be enfolded—as if you were talking to each one of them. Laughton could do it. Sinatra and Judy Garland have done it. I try to do it by placing my *imaginary* audience on the fourth wall as primary objects, or in conjunction with the dim shapes of people in any area of the auditorium where I *cannot* make direct eye contact with an actual member of the audience. (When you were in the audience, have you ever been visually contacted by a performer? Didn't you feel self-conscious, uncomfortable, abused? If you were sweet, you tried to guess what was expected of you, and perhaps played back with facial reactions. If you were annoyed, you probably made a stony face, or yawned into the actor's face, or simply adjusted your clothing in misery—feeling you were being used.) In a night club or in vaudeville, performers often make direct use of a member of the audience (at his expense), but if he talks back, the performer can improvise on it, or out of it, or take it further. In plays, too, as in everything, there are exceptions when the play demands that you cope with shifting realities or the director makes the character's task a direct confrontation with the given audience or a member of it. Occasionally, your character might have to ask for a specific response from the living audience; or the character may be asked to step out of the play and out of the character for an interlude with the existing audience. But these are the rare exceptions.

To return to the rule: remember that your character's dialogue with the audience is written down, that it must stay in the time and place of the character, and must be alive as it is sent to your imagined audience whom you have put around, in back of, and between yourself and the actual audience so that they will feel included, and enchanted, but not put upon!

ACCENTS AND DIALECTS

If I have to play a character with a foreign accent or a regional dialect, I consult a specialist, and with the help I'm given by my good ear (thank God) and my knowledge of the phonetic alphabet, I work around the clock on the sounds and rhythm of my new speech pattern. I get records of it so I can listen all day. I go to films where people talk the way I am supposed to. I make my friends and family the victims of my continuous practicing. I try to speak with my new speech pattern until it becomes second nature, until I stop hearing myself or checking myself. I try to do it *long* before I get to the words of the play, because if I practice it immediately or exclusively on the lines of my part, I will set line readings that can't be undone; I will test my words for sound rather than meaning, and do my character irrevocable damage.

Even my husband was a little shocked when I went, as a replacement, into *The Deep Blue Sea* and was introduced to an almost completely British cast and immediately spoke to them with a British accent ("What a nerve!"). They may even have laughed at me, and I wouldn't have blamed them, but the point was that they *didn't* laugh when I came to rehearsing and playing my part with them. The transition into Hester's language was all prepared for. I recommend this practice whether it be Russian, Chinese, Scotch or New England—whatever the accent or dialect may be.

There is an interesting psychological difference for the character if he is speaking in another language than his own with an accent, or if he has the local dialect of his origin—his childhood. Remember that if you have a foreign accent, you are trying *not* to have it. You are trying to overcome it and to speak the new language beautifully. (A Rumanian friend of mine, on hearing herself on a tape recorder, asked, "Who eez dat wooman?" and I had to say, "That's you." She said, "Dunt bee seely, dat wooman has an ahksent!") If on the other hand, your character has a regional dialect, "you" are speaking in and dealing with the depths of "your" origins. Become familiar with another childhood with new sounds and melodies.

I also claim that if you don't have a perfect ear, once you have studied the speech pattern diligently, the result needn't be absolutely authentic as long as you have faith in it and *believe* that it springs from you in your role. (Laurette Taylor, in *The Glass Menagerie,* did not have an authentic southern speech, but she thought she did, so we believed it too!)

DRESSING THE PART—THE COSTUME AND MAKEUP

An eyelash, a mustache, a wig, the shoes, even padding put on for a role must become an integral part of you. They ought to free the new "you" wholly. Everything must be developed for its sensory effect on you, the character. I think an anecdote about Alfred Lunt tells the story. He was working on *The Guardsman* by Molnar. In the course of the comedy, the character he was going to play wants to test his wife's fidelity by pretending to be a Russian officer and attempting, in this guise, to seduce her. (Mr. Lunt had to find the truth of his character's dress and makeup *plus* the reality of his disguise which had to convince everyone that he was that Russian officer.) He didn't see how it was possible to fool one's own wife, or anyone really close, with a physical disguise and accent. So he worked very hard on both and tested them against life. In a *modified* costume he paid a visit to his neighborhood grocer with whom he was on good terms, and whom he saw and talked to almost daily. He spoke to him in character with his accent. The grocer didn't recognize him. Mr. Lunt was secure about his homework.

MORAL STANDARDS

If you should feel schizophrenic about attempting to stay an honest artist and worker in our present-day theater, for the health of your soul and mind, remember that what makes you an artist is your *private* domain, and you can try to stay an artist or develop into one. But also remember that it is your duty to function in the theater—and the theater *is* what it *is!* Only when you are functioning can you try to influence or make a better theater. Claim your place.

30

COMMUNICATION

WHEN all the work is done, every artist wants to communicate, no matter how much he may speak of "art for art's sake." The painter has not painted with the final goal of looking at his work *alone*. The writer wants readers. The musician wants to be heard. The actor must want to be seen and heard after he has created a new human being, and he wants his creation to be meaningful to that body of people sitting in the auditorium.

Confusion often sets in for the artist who wants to keep his integrity while he is working; knowing that at this point, he must not consider the effectiveness of his work or its popular reception. During the involvement with the creative stages, the work should always spring from his point of view and his integrity. The prayer that it will communicate, the inner urge that it will reach and convince many people should come later and not be a distraction en route. (The commercial tradesman may have a strong degree of skill, but he uses it, from beginning to end, for the purpose of marketing it as part of a consumer commodity.) We mustn't forget, however, that we went into the theater to offer ourselves and what we have to tell others, not solely to have a private experience. There is a fine line between immersing ourselves in our work needs and remembering that we are preparing an offering.

Sometimes, the actor may feel that if he works the way he has been trained, he will become *too* involved in his role. If you should ever actually forget that you are on a stage to the point of being totally unaware of being watched, you would be insane or in trauma. You would take off on your own and no longer be in the play. You might then be involved in what is called "psychodrama," which is sometimes used for the mentally disturbed. I insist that you can work for maximum involvement in the play, and yet be aware, with a part of you, if someone in the audience laughs in the right or wrong place; you will be aware if an audience gets restless or is spellbound, or if someone coughs on a crucial line. This is the sixth sense, or the extrasensory perception, of most actors. This is why I never teach playing *to* the audience or communicating with them for its own sake.

The way an audience reaches out to me when I am presenting a character who is alive on stage, the empathy and identification they have with me, I believe to be the true realm of the actor, rather than reaching out to them and hitting them over the head with my "interpretation," my "ideas," and my "intellectual choices" for the character. If an actor does that to me when I am in the audience, I always want to say, "I get it! I get it! Leave me alone!" As I said in the chapter on "Concept" (Chapter 1), this is my choice, and so, for "Communication," I want to emphasize it again.

Another interesting technical aspect is involved in communication. I have spoken about *revealing* the character—to strip to the soul of the character. In our daily lives, most of us protect our souls with a mask which covers us from exposure. The Englishman has his "stiff upper lip"; we have our own native social customs or family rules about covering the moments when our equilibrium is shaken by an event which touches our emotions. In life if someone insults us we actually may feel as if we'd been slapped in the face, but we find an almost instantaneous cover to adjust to it. We laugh or pretend it didn't matter, or we top him with another insult. If someone publicly expresses tenderness, and our heart melts, we look for an immediate mask to prove that we aren't softies, haven't been touched, and so we laugh or make a joke of it, or cover with nonchalance. But as an actor, in order to reveal what's at stake for the character on the deepest level and allow for pertinent communication with the audience, I must make myself, for ultimate expression, *more* vulnerable than in life. I want to remove the mask I might normally use as a cover. What you reveal and do when you are truly vulnerable and wounded is totally different from when, as in life, your purpose is, so often, to prove that you are invulnerable.

Projection of voice and body in the old-fashioned sense seems quite unnecessary to me. I am not referring to the outer technical problems of having a poorly produced, breathy or squeaky voice which must be corrected by a voice teacher, and which must be slavishly corrected by you, or blurred, messy articulation of sounds, which lies in the department of speech and must be similarly conquered. You will not be heard *if* your verbal actions are general and don't reach their mark on the actor's side of the footlights—*not* because they are not being sent into the audience.

High visibility is not achieved by upstaging another actor or looking for the brightest light in the playing area, but by the strength and clarity of your character's actions sent from the depth of your involvement in your life on stage. Clear, revealing actions are always seen and heard.

To be heard so intently that a pin dropping would be a

shock, to be seen as if you yourself would be radiating with light is, of course, the perfect high C of communication. But even on an average level, being heard and seen from your entrance to your exit must be sustained for true communication!

31

STYLE

Style is the dirtiest word in the actor's vocabulary. It belongs to critics, essayists and historians, and fits nowhere into a creative process. It is serviceable for catalogues and reference books. But in the act of creation, whether it be a baby or a role in a play, you cannot predetermine style (shape, sound or form).

The many reasons behind most actors' misunderstandings and inaccurate concern with style have made for a chain reaction of centuries of bad acting and empty, tedious, or just plain noisy theater. One reason is the actor's mistrust in his own instrument or ability to bring his own being into full play. Or he has an academic education which he is misusing. Or he has no education and is self-consciously employing empty formulas. A deep-rooted reason springs from the *stylized* productions we were taken to as children, which conditioned us to accept the "manner" of performing certain plays. For some of us, the conditioning is so strong that as we grow up, we neither question nor challenge these stenciled preconceptions so that we actually come to believe that predetermined styles for presentation are a necessary part-and-parcel of the play.

Style

Remember that all of the *labels* you are familiar with (realistic, surrealistic, romantic, satirical, farcical, tragi-comic, naturalistic, classical, neo-classical, avant-garde, theater of the absurd, theater of cruelty, etc.) were stuck onto a piece of work *after* it came into existence and not before. The beat and sound of "rock and roll" was made before someone named it. Works are categorized by observers, audiences and critics, but *not* the creators. Any concern you have for the "style" will immediately place you on the wrong side of the footlights.

To follow a fashion or borrow one from the past, to start with a concept of the outer form, the outer shape, the outer style, is a trap every artist in every art form should guard against like the fatal plague. To "create," according to Webster, is to bring into being, to cause to come into existence. It also means that a concept must arise from content. The shape of the wrapping or the package depends on what's inside. (Read Ben Shahn's extraordinary book, *The Shape of Content.* He is talking about painting, and every word should be an eye-opener for the actor. Read *On Modern Art* by Paul Klee.) In comparing painting to acting I used to say that to paint an apple you have to see and to sense everything about the apple before you can come to a statement about it, and that if you combined that statement with your skill you might produce a canvas that had your mark. Picasso claimed you have to *eat* the apple first. He clearly wanted to come to full grips with his material and digest it before he gave it shape, before his statement came into being.

In a play, the net result of the "style"—what the form, shape and sound will be—is a product of the director's concept of the playwrights' content expressed by the inner and outer life of the actor.

"How do I approach the differences between a comedy and a tragedy if I'm going to be a truthful actor?" (An equally simplistic question would be, "What's funny or sad in your life?") Again and again, an *honest* actor ignores the wisecracks his character makes in an attempt to avoid signaling "comedy." He has forgotten how much of his own life is spent wisecracking and *trying* to be funny, to amuse the people around him. If, as a character, he shows the *audience* how he wisecracks instead of proving his humor to the other character on stage, he is acting dishonestly.

What makes a fight between two people tragic, ugly, or funny? It is the cause of the fight, the objective of the fight, and the relationship between the fighters. Haven't you ever fought with someone you loved, even coming to physical violence, and in the middle of the battle realized it was funny? If there were real hatred in your relationship, the fight would be terrifying and ugly, and its consequence might be tragic.

If comedic material gets heavy or unfunny, the director or the actor, or both of them, have left out something inherent in the material. In Christopher Fry's one-act *A Phoenix Too Frequent,* a lady is discovered in her husband's tomb. She is mourning him, and wants to die so that she can join him in Hades. It is a deliciously funny play. A young actress always seems to be stymied about how to make the loss of the husband and her own death wish real to herself without playing tragedy. In attempting to bring the role to a proper life, she usually does not choose what really matters out of the total content of the play. Christopher Fry proposes that the phoenix, which arises from the ashes, all too frequently is a desire for life—procreation. While she is "mourning," the lady soon falls in love with a soldier, a guard who arrives in the middle of the night to find out why the tomb is lighted. The lady is a wild romantic, very middle class, and her "notion" of dying is in conflict with her human needs for comfort, warmth, food and drink, and making love and life.

The actress may also have forgotten that the deceased husband was obviously a giant bore who "made Homer sound like balance sheets." So if the actress has chosen a seeming death wish or the loss of her husband out of context and attempted to make them real to herself, she may be "truthful" on her own terms, probably tragically so, but not truthful to the play.

And so it goes, with the exploration of a particular apple or a specific play. You have to examine and digest the whole thing and make it yours. You cannot reshape it to suit your most convenient needs or violate the playwright's intentions and content if you don't want to be accused by a critic or an observer of having "no style."

If a director and a group of actors would have a full experience with the content of *Awake and Sing, Rocket to the Moon,* and *The Country Girl,* they would *arrive* at three different "styles" in their productions, although all three plays were written by Odets. But if they began by working for an "Odetsian style," they would come up with an empty package. I believe the same things to be true for Shakespeare or Goethe or Molière or Shaw or Chekhov or Ibsen or O'Neill or Beckett or Ionesco or Brecht or . . .

From the outset, I have attempted to break down all the areas in which you can work and search for realities in yourself which serve the character and the play. These closing statements are simply a reminder to avoid falling into the many pitfalls of starting from the outside in. Avoid the "manner of . . . !" Avoid the cliché! Above all, in both rehearsals and in performance, avoid *commenting* on the play, or the character, or the circumstances, or the symbols, or the message. Put your instincts and sense of truth, your understanding of human realities to use while probing and grappling with the content and the roots of the material. Be specific and real in your actions, and they will communicate your artistic statement. Bring your universal understanding of the present *to* the present. Serve your country as a real artist.

Art Skill and contrivance in adapting natural things to man's use.

Artist One who professes and practices an art in which conception and execution are governed by imagination and taste.

EPILOGUE

THE PROFESSION of acting has been maligned throughout the ages. The actor has been considered foolish not only when he was clowning on stage but even for having chosen to be an actor—a vagabond or hobo strolling through life without importance or worth. He has been denied burial ground and has been accused of prostitution and other varieties of immorality, egomania, vanity, ruthlessness, hypocrisy, toadyism, to name a few. Even when his gifts were recognized as extraordinary, his talent was looked upon as an accident of nature. When the public turned him into an idol, they treated him like some rare species behind bars. They poked into his private life and examined every detail of it with the audacity and curiosity they might have exhibited while watching monkeys at their most intimate moments in the zoo.

To a degree, we are to blame for this opinion of ourselves. In our longing for dignity, we have not followed through in our work to merit respect for our profession and respect for our own work in that profession.

I believe that we should begin with the realization that

acting entails a craft as subtle and delicate as the most demanding creative art. Humanism is at the root of it. A crucial social offering is in the making. Consistently good acting is never an accident or empty of this purpose. To achieve a technique which will allow for a genuine existence on stage can take a lifetime to accomplish. The search never stops; there are no dead ends. If we pursue this search, many of the humiliations to which we are subjected become meaningless. Success and failure become a fascinating struggle to be evaluated by the individual actor in conjunction with his own awareness of the work at hand.

To bring to an audience the revelation of the failings and aspirations, the dreams and desires, the negative and the positive aspects of human beings—this is what we should set as our goal as committed theater artists. Then we will be respected and have respect for ourselves and respect for acting!

INDEX

INDEX

INDEX